# SINGING WITH MIND, BODY, AND SOUL

# SINGING
## WITH
# MIND & BODY
# SOUL

*A Practical Guide for Singers*
*and Teachers of Singing*

Betty Jeanne Chipman
With Joseph Hoffman and Sara Thomas

wheat/mark

*Singing with Mind, Body, and Soul: A Practical Guide for Singers and Teachers of Singing*

Design: Jamie Chipman
Illustrations: Jonathan Hoffman
Vocalise notation: Joseph Hoffman

Published by Wheatmark®
610 East Delano Street, Suite 104
Tucson, Arizona 85705 U.S.A.
www.wheatmark.com

**Publisher's Cataloging-In-Publication Data**
(Prepared by The Donohue Group, Inc.)

Chipman, Betty Jeanne.
Singing with mind, body, & soul : a practical guide for singers and teachers of singing / by Betty Jeanne Chipman ; with Joseph Hoffman and Sara Thomas ; foreword by JoAnn Ottley.

   p. : ill., music ; cm.

   Includes bibliographical references and index.
   ISBN: 978-1-60494-089-3

1. Singing—Instruction and study—Handbooks, manuals, etc. 2. Voice culture.
3. Singing—Methods. 4. Singers—Training of. I. Hoffman, Joseph (Joseph M.), 1976-
II. Thomas, Sara, 1973- III. Ottley, Jo Ann. IV. Title. V. Title: Singing with mind, body, and soul : a practical guide for singers and teachers of singing

MT820 .C45 2008
783.04                              2008928902

# DEDICATION

*To my son Jamie.*
*Without his encouragement,*
*help and talent,*
*this book would never have been published.*

*Also, to my students,*
*my "musical children,"*
*who have taught me so much.*

*"As a choral director, it is impossible to overstate my excitement with what I continue to learn from* Singing with Mind, Body, and Soul. *It documents the approaches and exercises used and refined so successfully by Betty Jeanne Chipman over the years in her attempt to 'free the voice' to 'allow it to sing.' We now have the treasure of all that she has learned, experienced, and synthesized in her illustrious career as a highly successful voice teacher. I have for years admired her teaching. She is one of the finest teachers of voice anywhere. Now her legacy will live on long past even our own years. I can't imagine anyone who studies or teaches voice—including choral conductors—being without this book."*

—Dr. Ronald Staheli, Head of Choral Studies, Brigham Young University

*"Often even the most well-meaning vocal coach or teacher may focus on short term gains for the sake of style, performance, or competition. Unfortunately, if not kept in perspective, the goal of a life-long pursuit of singing may be sacrificed. Betty Jeanne Chipman's many years of expert care of hundreds of singers is capsulized in this book and captures the importance of building a vocally healthy approach to teaching. The careful adoption of the principals and techniques laid out in this text will improve the overall vocal quality, reduce or eliminate vocal tension, and provide the student with the joy of a life of singing without vocal injury. Outlined in these pages is not only a philosophy of vocal pedagogy, but also a practical guide detailing vocalizes and techniques, explaining their usefulness and intent."*

–Harlan R. Muntz, M.D., Faye M. Muntz, M.M., Singing Voice Specialist

*"It has been my good fortune to be present at many of Betty Jeanne's lessons and to accompany some of her most outstanding students. This book is a treasure trove of method and inspiration from one of the most successful teachers of this generation."*

–Bonnie L. Goodliffe, Mormon Tabernacle Organist

*"Betty Jeanne has been an asset of incalculable value to our artistic community, and I have been thrilled as I listened to her students' performances and recordings."*

—Clive Romney, Recording Engineer, Musician

# TABLE OF CONTENTS

# ACKNOWLEDGMENTS

The first person I must acknowledge is Joseph Hoffman. Without him this book would never have been written. Although many students recommended that I compile and put in at least a booklet form my concepts of teaching singing, I doubt that I would have taken the time to do so.

I am especially grateful to my son, Jamie, for his design and art and for all of his support and suggestions as he read the chapters many times while preparing the manuscript for publication. Thanks to Sara Thomas, who is not only an excellent writer and editor, but also is a fine singer and has contributed much to clarifying the flow of the book as it was merged with Joseph's scholarly paper. Thanks to Joseph, Sara, and Jamie for making my life's work accessible to teachers, directors, and performers.

I must acknowledge the National Association of Teachers of Singing for the many years of conventions and workshops that have enabled us to learn from the master teachers who have so generously given their time. Our Utah NATS chapter meetings have been invaluable both for bringing so many master teachers to us as well as the meetings where we learn from each other. We have a wonderful, supportive community of teachers of singing who are willing to share their knowledge.

Thanks too, to the music faculty of Brigham Young University and especially to Joseph's committee, for accepting his compilation of my work. I also thank my colleagues at the University of Utah, where I taught for 30 years, for their friendship and support. Also, I thank my many students. As the song says, "By your students you'll be taught." I have learned much from each of you as I hope you have learned from me.

I am very grateful for the encouragement and endorsements of those who read our manuscript. They include, JoAnn Ottley, former vocal coach for the Mormon Tabernacle Choir; Dr. Ronald Staheli, head of choral studies at Brigham Young University; Dr. Craig Jessop, former director of the Mormon Tabernacle Choir; Faye Muntz, vocal specialist and Harlan Muntz, M.D., pediatric otolaryngologist and professor at the University of Utah Voice Disorder Clinic; Iain McKay, former director of the Temple Square

Concert Series and his wife Heidi; and Bonnie Goodliffe, Mormon Tabernacle Organist. A special thanks to Carla Wood, former owner/editor and creator of *Classical Singer* magazine, who, before her untimely death, gave me much encouragement and help. JoAnn Ottley was kind enough to write the foreword.

I also thank my students, especially Jaimee Belnap Gabrielsen, who edited the choral chapter, and Becky Alexander, who added insight as she read each chapter with me. Other students who read it and made valuable suggestions are Ivalani Bradshaw, Rebecca Hample, Janilyn Anderson, Clara Hurtado Lee, and Erin McComber, who also helped with the index. I also thank Rebecca Wilcox Wilberg for her comments. A special thanks to my wonderful accompanists, Becky Alexander, Cheryl Nielsen, Kathy Skidmore, Denise Farrington, Alan Eastman, and many others who have played in my studio for so many years. My gratitude to Michael Chipman, Susan Goodfellow, and Darwin Thomas for proofreading the manuscript and to my son Rob for his encouragement and help with the final reading.

# INTRODUCTION
## by Joseph Hoffman

Several years ago, when I was faced with vocal problems that neither I nor voice teachers nor doctors were able to solve, a trusted mentor suggested that I contact Betty Jeanne Chipman for voice lessons. I hesitated—her studio was an hour's drive from my home. Couldn't I find someone closer? When a second person independently made the same suggestion, I decided to act. I called, and she agreed to take me as a student. My vocal problems up to that point had been so persistent, mysterious, and demoralizing, that I despaired of ever correcting them. When I began with Betty Jeanne (as she is affectionately called by students and colleagues), I felt her calm but firm faith that we would work through the problem and I would be able to sing beautifully again without pain or discomfort. I had become so anxious and distressed about my singing, and even though I had a hard time believing that things could get better, I was able to rely on her steadiness and persistence. In lessons she didn't waste any time getting right to the heart of my vocal problems. Once we had identified the problems, I found she was equipped with a wealth of teaching tools and vocal exercises to help me undo the problems and find a new freedom in my voice. I was comforted and reassured by her attitude of not being in a hurry to fix me. She was willing to take all the time necessary for my body to get the message she and I were trying to send it.

Very soon I recognized that I was working with a master teacher. This gracious and youthful-spirited woman (she was 82 when I first met her) has spent her life steadily absorbing all the vocal science, wisdom, and teaching tools she could possibly discover. The first time I realized the depth of her dedication to a lifetime of pursuing vocal knowledge was when I heard her casually comment in reference to a particular book on vocal technique, "I think I should read that one again." A few weeks later, I found out she had followed through on her resolution.

Even in her eighties, she continues to learn, consider, and experiment with new ideas. She often points out to her students, "By your pupils you will be taught." I have also heard her say, "The day I stop learning is the day I should quit teaching."

Far from being a mere imitator of other people's ideas, however, Betty Jeanne takes the best information she can find, then evaluates, adapts, and makes it her own. Many of the techniques in this book are based on ideas she has gleaned from a variety of sources: books, observations of other voice teachers, workshops, and students. Most of these ideas were picked up so long ago and have gone through so many revisions and adaptations that it is now impossible to cite or give credit to the original source. At the same time, Betty Jeanne and I—together with the help of Sara Thomas—have made every effort to cite sources whenever possible.

Somewhere along the way of reconstructing my voice, I realized that here was the perfect topic for my scholarly paper required for the completion of my master's degree in choral conducting from Brigham Young University. If someone did not take the time to document Betty Jeanne's teaching techniques (and she made it clear that she never would herself), eventually they would be lost and forgotten. For me—and I believe for many others—this would have been a tragic loss.

I approached Betty Jeanne about this idea, and she was very supportive and enthusiastic. She gave me access to all of her formal and informal writings about singing and teaching singing. She also permitted me to observe lessons taught in her private studio. During 2003 and 2004 I observed and documented about one-hundred one-hour voice lessons taught in her home. Additionally we conducted several one-on-one interviews during which time I was able to clarify many concepts I observed in her teaching and to probe a little more deeply into certain issues. As I began the writing process, Betty Jeanne carefully read over my work multiple times, often making corrections and suggestions.

The scholarly paper was finished and submitted in April 2005, and perhaps that would have been a great place to stop. As it turned out, the completion of my paper was just the beginning of what has developed into a much larger collaborative project culminating in this book. Betty Jeanne set to work writing additional chapters that more than doubled the content of my scholarly paper. Sara Thomas then came on board, taking on the task of merging my paper with Betty Jeanne's new material. This all culminated in the present book.

For the sake of clarity, we decided that the first person "I" always represents Betty Jeanne's voice despite the co-authorship. This seemed appropriate since she is the author of the ideas. If no source is indicated for the quotes, Betty Jeanne herself is the source. Many quotes are little gems that I record- ed while observing her teach. In addition, we decided to use the pronoun "he" for the student and the pronoun "she" for the teacher when describing them in generic terms to avoid the cumbersome "he/she" alternative.

This book was always intended to take a practical approach to singing. Delving into the science and physiology of singing has been avoided except where it had a direct and practical application. Most chapter topics are com- bined with vocal exercises and teaching tools that form the heart of this book. These constitute the core of Betty Jeanne Chipman's teaching method and may be adapted to the reader's own use. In Appendix 2, most of the vocal exercises presented in this book are compiled in a compact form to provide quick and easy reference. Don't expect to fully reap the benefits of the exercises found in the appendix without referring to the individual chap- ters where detailed instructions about their use can be found.

As far as my voice is concerned, I am pleased to say that I have made excel- lent progress working with Betty Jeanne. She has helped me to discover, among other things, a way of singing that involves less tension in the jaw and throat. A more resonant, vibrant tone has been the result. All involved in this project deeply hope that this compilation of Betty Jeanne's teaching techniques will provide readers with new insights and ideas for their own singing or teaching of singing.

# FOREWORD
by JoAnn Ottley

The world loves its singers. Whether on the big stages of the world or in the local church, there is a fascination about singing and singers that goes beyond normal human interest. The musical sound that emanates from the throat of a singer—what has been called the "acoustic fingerprint of the soul"—can carry an impact, sometimes transformative, for the listener.

The often unsung heroes of the singer's world claim far less recognition, far less curiosity. Those who know "the rest of the story," however, recognize that there should be medals, fanfares, and trumpeted gratitude for that crucial other force in the singer's life: those who successfully shape, guide, comfort, and endure the preparation of those singers.

Teachers of singing, as in every other human category, come in all varieties, and the extremity of the art form being what it is, the teachers' own extremes, for good or ill, will show up in their teaching. A few years of bad training can go on forever for a singer. But so can a few years of excellent, healthful training endure and provide a foundation for a lifetime of choices in the singing world. Some teachers seem to have a mold into which a singer is expected to fit. Others seem able to mold to the singer, take the ingredients offered, shape the package accordingly, and free the singer to fly.

As vocal coach of the Mormon Tabernacle Choir for decades, it was my duty to participate in all auditions (many hundreds of them) of choir hopefuls. That has been a tremendous observatory for hearing the products of various vocal studios. Betty Jeanne Chipman has been a friend and a colleague throughout my professional life, so I was always particularly aware of her students, whether current or past, who came through those auditions. Betty Jeanne's students were the ones able to "fly." They were, almost without exception, those we could count on—voices which had not been pushed, which were free, not extreme in any way, but healthy and balanced. Some had stayed in small, supportive vocal situations, and some had climbed the heights of singer accomplishment. Many from her studio have become highly accomplished nationally and internationally recognized singers.

For many years I have referred to Betty Jeanne as the "Mother Superior of Voice Teachers," and that friendly title is not lightly bestowed. She knows the science and she knows how to transmit it. Her mantra is "free the voice." But perhaps overriding all of this, her students are as nourished in their souls as in their voices. She has some magic to offer. What more could we ask?

SINGING WITH MIND, BODY, AND SOUL

# 1
# Singing and the Mind, Body, Soul Connection

*"The soul longs to dwell with the body."*
—Leonardo da Vinci

*"Singing is the highest expression of music because it is the most
direct expression of the emotions of the soul."*
—Clara Kathleen Rogers

*"'Know thyself' applies to the singer more than to other professions,
because to sing well, body, soul, and mind are tuned together to do it."*
—Giovanni Battista Lamperti

*"It is your mind, not your body, that is musical or unmusical."*

*"You must have the perfect quality in mind or you will not sing it."*

*"I have spent my days stringing and unstringing my instrument,
while the song I came to sing remains unsung."*
—Rabindranath Tagore

*"Psychological complexes are more difficult to overcome than
physiological misfits are to adjust."*
—G.B. Lamperti

Every teacher lives for those "a-ha" moments when a student truly grasps a
correct concept of vocal technique. I love to hear comments like, "Wow!
That feels so good, I didn't know I had so much space in the back of my

throat." Or, "When I open up and feel more back space, my voice feels more forward, but when I try to put it forward, it feels tight in my throat." Or, "That's cool. I can really feel the vowels change, but I'm not doing anything to make it happen."

In contrast, I have also heard comments like these from singers over the years:

- "My voice gets so tired when I sing."

- "I get so nervous when I sing solos. How do I get over stage fright?"

- "Singing used to be so much fun. It isn't anymore."

- "It feels like I'm not working hard enough."

- "I feel like I have to tense something to start the tone."

- "I don't like to listen to myself on a tape recording."

- "Judges always say I have too much vibrato."

- "My throat hurts when I sing."

I believe that the root of these and many other vocal problems lies in the disconnection—and at times dysfunction—of the mind, body, and soul. Each has a specific role, and the most rewarding singing involves all three. The children's song by Janeen Brady perhaps says it best: "You think it; you feel it; you do it." While the song speaks simply of the role imagination plays in our daily lives, it also applies to singing. To "think it" uses the mind, to "feel it" uses the soul, and to "do it" uses the body.

Teaching singing is not an exact science. Many of the mental imagery and suggestions we use cannot be proven by a scientific formula. Yet what we teach must be based on sound knowledge of the physiological and psychological aspects of the vocal instrument. Vital in the process is knowing how the subconscious and conscious minds work, understanding how each individual student's mind processes the information, and helping the singer get the message from the mind to the body without excluding the soul.

## Getting Into the Mind of the Singer

"Every book worth reading is a meeting place. Some would call it a battle-
ground: are the writer's ideas or the reader's preconceptions to survive?"[1] So
it is with the student-teacher relationship. Each student comes to us with a
preconceived idea of what they must do to sing based on their previous
instruction and experience, and then has to determine whether the new way
or the old way is to remain. What a previous teacher has taught the singer
can greatly influence how he perceives and interprets instruction from a new
teacher, so much so that the student can be asking his voice and body to do
the opposite of what the teacher hopes to communicate. Thus, when we
start teaching a new student we need to understand how he is interpreting
the instruction we are giving him. How often I have wished I could peer
into the mind of a student and see how he is processing the concepts I am
explaining to him.

In most cases, by allowing the student to describe his mental imagery and
kinesthetic sensation and carefully listening as he does so, we are able to get
a view of his thinking. Asking the student to describe the new sensation in
his own words also helps to reinforce his awareness.

E. Herbert-Caesari, one of the most accepted authorities on teaching the
old Italian style of singing, described the dilemma of vocal teachers: how to
get inside the mind of the student and help him to use his conscious and
subconscious minds effectively in singing.

> The subconscious mind knows exactly what to do, and how to do it.
> The conscious mind does not and will always mess up the voice if
> given the slightest chance. The conscious mind…*thinks* he knows,
> but doesn't. There will always be under his guidance, too much
> "beef" coupled to excess breath pressure, *forced* breath pressure,
> which starts the tone off heavily and roughly, and after that he will
> assuredly give the resultant sound column the wrong direction, *forcing*
> it everywhere except in the right channel. No, once and for all, the
> conscious mind's job is to give orders, and orders alone. *Not* to do.
> After the order has been given there must be the *will* to do that
> order, and that is the work for the subconscious mind only…So the
> whole business boils down to that old Italian saying "*Let the cords
> sing.*" Don't interfere with it. If it goes wrong in some detail, the
> consciously given order may be defective or lacking.[2]

Herbert-Caesari's theory is that the conscious mind would get in the way and try to physically adjust the muscles because it would use local effort in the process. The conscious mind can be directed and learn what orders to give, but it cannot execute these orders because it would apply them physically. It can be trained to accept what is right, but it cannot do the work so it passes on its orders to the subconscious mind which knows instinctively what to do. A natural singer lets his voice sing. The teacher must allow the natural singer to obey his instincts as well as help him to establish a secure, dependable technique.

The following exercise[3] shows the process of getting into the subconscious mind (for the complete exercise, see Chapter 7, Exercise 7a). While thinking the words below in your mind and reading only the underlined vowels aloud, allow the vowels to migrate from one to the next. The conscious mind gets out of the way because it is involved in looking at the words. The subconscious mind is then able to take over and automatically make the instinctive, physical adjustments for the different vowels. As one is looking at the vowels, the subconscious mind is only thinking the vowels, not consciously shaping them. The singer feels the different shapes of the vowels without physically making it happen.

F<u>a</u>ther
P<u>a</u>w
<u>A</u>h
S<u>o</u>rry
Sc<u>o</u>tch
<u>O</u>h
P<u>o</u>lite
R<u>o</u>se
M<u>oo</u>n

As this exercise takes effect, it makes the singer aware of the muscles of the throat and pharynx releasing and warming the tone. Every time the larynx goes into the free, lowered, and balanced posture it helps to train the muscles of the vocal tract to release tension.

**The Mind and Body Connection**

Sometimes by giving too much verbal instruction as teachers, we inadvertently contribute to the conscious mind doing what the subconscious mind should do. If a singer's mind is cluttered with all kinds of instructions, it is very likely he will try to make his voice sing, rather than let his voice sing. A teacher's primary role should be to guide the student to greater self-awareness of his body and his singing habits, empowering the student to be his own teacher and make his own corrections.

The first step in correcting a vocal problem is often simply noticing and recognizing what is really happening with the body. Then the body needs to repeatedly *feel* what it is like to sing correctly. Only then can the correct way of singing become a habit. One of the major goals of this book is to present and explain specific tools for helping the body to *feel* what it is like to sing with freedom and for increasing the kinesthetic (body/physical) awareness while singing.

As the mind notices things through objective and non-judgmental observation, the body can easily and naturally correct any problems. For example, you can tell a novice singer again and again that he needs to drop his jaw more, or you can simply have him observe in a mirror what he is doing. The singer thinks, "Oh! I thought I was dropping my jaw." He then instantly fixes it. The informed mind tells the voice and body what to do. The teacher's job is to get the right concept and information to the student's mind.

Many students work too hard, thinking they must use a lot of intense energy when they sing. Good singing should feel natural and easy. When singing begins to feel like it requires a lot of muscular effort, the conscious mind has gotten too involved. Then it is time to remember: "Let it happen. Don't make it happen."

When students have the tendency to work too hard, I often ask them to sing their favorite childhood song or a simple folk song. They usually let the voice sing easily and don't try to make their voice sound big or impressive. Recently a student was singing "The Singer" by Michael Head. I suggested her approach was too operatic and asked her to sing it like a minstrel, more in the ballad style. The difference was amazing. Her voice was warm and expressive instead of heavy and contrived.

Once a student with an advanced degree in vocal performance came to me for lessons because he struggled with tension problems and vocal fatigue. He was working so hard physically to sing—vigorously pulling in his abdominal muscles, laboriously shaping his face and mouth. It was simply exhausting to him, besides causing strain on his voice. I suggested to him that he was working much too hard and paying too high a price for the results he was getting. We then worked to help him discover and monitor his own habits of excess muscular activity. Basically, we needed to get his mind to stop giving so many instructions and instead play the role of observer. By having him place a hand on his abdomen, for example, he began to feel just how much he was pulling in and tightening. I suggested that he simply allow the tone to activate the breathing muscles. The breathing mechanism naturally and instinctively supplied sufficient breath energy without him consciously tightening his abdominal muscles. We worked other exercises as well that helped his mind to quiet down and encouraged his body to sing with a natural ease. After several lessons he had made remarkable progress and declared, "I feel like I have a new voice. It has never felt this good to sing!"

**Using the Singing Tools to Connect the Body and Mind**
Each vocal exercise in this book has a specific purpose. The real value of these exercises is that they train the right habits of singing. They are designed to help your body feel what it is like to sing with muscular freedom. Muscles have a strong "memory" of their usual way of doing things. Thus, when trying to undo habits of muscular tension, you should use the most efficient methods possible to accelerate the process of helping the muscles to "forget" the old way and habituate the new way.

Often these exercises involve the use of a physical tool designed to help the conscious mind get the message to the subconscious mind by causing the right sensations to happen. For example, sometimes I ask a student to use his index fingers to gently press in at the corners of the mouth while singing an [ɑ] vowel to help the jaw feel a complete release (see Exercise 5a, Chapter

5). Another tool that helps the jaw learn to release is to place a cork between the back molars (see Chapter 5). In other situations, the tool is no more than a hand or a finger resting on a certain part of the body to monitor for tension.

These tools speed the learning process because they provide immediate kinesthetic feedback for the singer. They help the singer feel the difference between a free flowing, ringing tone, uninhibited by muscular tension, and a tone that is made by wrongly tensing the muscles, such as the muscles of the torso or the muscles of the vocal tract—especially the tongue and mylohyoid muscle. Used together with the exercises in this book, the tools allow the vocal mechanism, tongue, jaw, abdominal muscles, and the entire body to release tension.

## Connecting the Soul

When we focus too much on technique—which in time will become more automatic—we can become overly anxious about every little sound, resulting in both unwanted muscular tension and the disconnection of the soul. Vocal problems will frequently disappear when a teacher gives the student permission to stop worrying about technique and just *sing*. I sometimes ask a student to pretend that they are an opera singer. When we imitate a sound, we usually become less inhibited and just let it happen. The tone most often becomes freer, warmer, and more beautiful. This spontaneity allows the subconscious mind to follow the intent to "ham it up," which in turn causes the throat to release and open, resulting in a more resonant sound because the lowered, balanced posture of the larynx creates a longer resonating column in the pharynx. The new openness and added space allows the tone to radiate upward and causes the "ring" of the voice. The student, after trying this exercise and feeling the more resonant sound, often responds, "Did all of that sound come from me?"

In the last two or three decades, much research has been done in the field of music therapy and the healing qualities of music as it relates to resonance and sound. Part of this healing power lies in the fact that the voice resonates throughout our entire bodies. If we are in tune with the vibratory sensations, we can feel the vibration from our head to our toes. Tune into this sensation by putting your hand on the top of your head as you sing or do the lip buzz, and observe the vibration. Then put your hand on your sternum, and observe that in the lower register there is a deeper vibration in the chest.

My friend and colleague JoAnn Ottley, who has spent many years studying the healing power of the voice, describes this resonant quality of the voice:

> The idea of the voice as a healer is not new. It is rather ancient, and might most accurately be classified among the valuable things we've forgotten in our quest for scientific measurement. The paradox lies now in the fact that a clear understanding of the power of the human voice to heal comes directly from physics and our expanded concepts about the universe, which at the fundamental level could be said to *be* music. There is no requirement for faith nor belief, but only observation of results, now easily explained scientifically...The human voice may be the best tool available for reconciling the internal and external components of our beings. It works with the *breath*, and with *vibration*, the fundamental elements of our lives. It is available to all, without cost, and requires no expertise. Anyone who can groan or hum can claim the powerful benefits offered by the human voice. The body acts as something of a "sounding board," responding to the influences of the sound, and most especially the sound of the human voice.[4]

The exercises train the body and mind to work as a team. Then, as singing with the intent to express a true inner emotion or feeling connects the soul, wonderful things happen to the voice. Not only is the voice freer and more beautiful, it also reflects the mental, emotional, and physical nature of the singer, linking the personality of the individual to the song and carrying it to the heart of the listener. Olivea Dewhurst-Maddock describes how that connection between the voice and the soul has the power to heal:

> The voice reflects the mental, emotional, and physical condition of a person. It is truly a parable of the soul. In the same way that the soul links the personality of the individual to the whole...the voice links the smaller wave or particle of energy to the energy of the universe...In short, improve the use of your voice and you will start to feel better.[5]

Wouldn't it be a grand surprise if we found that within our own beings, our own breath, our own unique voices, lies waiting a superb power for healing, for helping us gently toward wholeness, and for uniting us with one another and more fully with ourselves?[6]

As teachers of singing, we need to be very aware of the mind, body, and soul of the singer. Always try to keep in tune with each student's needs. Always approach the corrections you give from a positive standpoint remembering that you are working with not just the physical voice, but also the soul of the singer.

I like to devote the first portion of each lesson to establishing good singing habits through specific exercises, then spend the remainder of the lesson singing appropriate literature. While singing literature, it is still important to monitor the technique and reinforce what was worked on during the exercises. However, I try and use the time singing literature to focus less on technique, and more on interpretation and expressing the music.

It is important to let students sing through an entire song, unless something is really not working well, so they have the experience of getting into the music and text and connecting their soul to singing. I remember one incident with a wonderful young singer who had stopped studying with me for a time while finishing a degree. When she returned to renew her study she said, "It feels so good to actually sing through an entire song. In my lessons at the university I was stopped after every few measures for every minute detail. Then the teacher and the pianist would disagree and they would spend the next fifteen minutes of my lesson arguing to make their point." She wasn't able to sing through an entire aria or song for the two years she studied there. Students come to their lessons to sing. True, expressive singing must be given time to connect with the soul.

Students enter the studio each week with such a variety of challenges and emotional highs and lows, as well as the stress of everyday living. Often just singing and working with wonderful music gives an outlet for the release of frustrations and tension. I will never forget a young student who was singing the lovely little art song set to Emily Dickinson's poem "This Little Rose." The last sentence reads, "Ah, little rose, how easy, for such as thee to die."

At the end of the song the student had tears in her eyes. I commented on the emotion that she felt for the poem. She responded, "My mother died last night." I had known her mother. I was nearly overcome to think that she would come to her lesson under such a condition of sadness. She told me, "I just needed to sing." At a time of such deep loss, singing helped her with the grieving and healing process. I was so glad that I had not stopped her to correct a little wrong interval, but allowed her the experience of singing from her soul.

---

1. I.A. Richards, as quoted in the foreword of Richard DeYoung's book *The Singer's Art: An Analysis of Vocal Principles.*
2. Herbert-Caesari, *Vocal Truth,* 30.
3. Adapted from Herbert-Caesari's *Vocal Truth,* 77.
4. Quoted with the author's permission from unpublished presentation materials.
5. Olivea Dewhurst-Maddock, *The Book of Sound Therapy,* 37.
6. It is beyond the scope of this book to go more deeply into this subject. For more information, I recommend the books *The 7 Secrets of Sound Healing,* by Jonathan Goldman and *The Book of Sound Therapy,* by Olivea Dewhurst-Maddock. See the Bibliography for complete references

# 2
# Posture and Muscle Releasing

*"Good posture precedes good breathing and singing."*

*"We learn by doing, not by theorizing."*

Every musical instrument must be played with a correctly balanced posture. The singing voice is no exception. Since singing involves the entire body, singers must work to maintain a posture free of tension that keeps the right relationship between the head, neck, and torso.

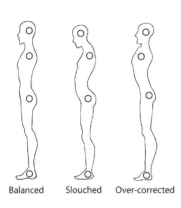

Balanced    Slouched    Over-corrected

*Figure 2.1*

To some people the word "posture" implies holding the body in one ideal position. This faulty mental concept produces rigid muscles and interferes with healthy singing. For this reason, teachers of the Alexander Technique (see Chapter 16) prefer to use the word "balance" in place of "posture." Balance implies that the skeletal frame does most of the work of resisting gravity and holding the body upright, leaving the muscles free to move the body through space as necessary. When the skeletal frame is misaligned and out of balance, the muscles have to do extra work to keep the body from falling over. Movement becomes effortful, strained, and awkward. Likewise in singing, if the body is out of balance, the muscles have to compensate, and singing becomes more labored and strained (see fig. 2.1).

As we discover a balanced relationship between head, neck, trunk, hips, and feet, our bodies acquire a feeling of lightness and ease of movement. There is an awareness of overall flexibility, greater freedom in the action of our eyes, less tension in the jaw, more relaxation in the tongue and throat, and deeper breathing. We feel a sense of weightlessness and can move our arms and legs with less effort.

A singer with a unique and beautiful color to her voice came to me for lessons. She had been taught to hold her body in a forced, firm, and high posture resulting in tension through the shoulders, neck, tongue, jaw, and forehead. Her inhalation and exhalation were also labored and this unnecessary tension caused her voice to be heavy, unwieldy, and often flat in pitch. While the root of her problem was in her overly tense inhalation and exhalation, we first worked to free and balance her posture. She now describes her posture as "high but flexible." With proper body alignment, she has been able to find a natural, free breathing process. Her innately beautiful vocal color is even more beautiful now with the added lightness and agility.

Like this singer, we must develop a "kinesthetic awareness" to establish and maintain a balanced posture and alert us to tensions or pressures in our bodies. As we notice tension, we send the mental instruction to our muscles to "let go." When we achieve habitual balanced posture, the singing tone becomes more vibrant, free, and resonant as a result of the muscular freedom and release.

As you perform the following exercises, allow your mind to take the role of quiet observer. Notice how releasing tensions in various areas of your body affects your posture, balance, and breathing. Allow the body to discover and experience a new, deeper feeling of release.

## <u>2a</u>
## Shoulder Releasing

- Imagine that a magic thread attached to the upper tip of the shoulder is lifting your right shoulder.

- Let it go up as high as it will go, while letting your arm hang loosely, like a dead-weight, close to your body.

- Suddenly release and let the shoulder drop.

- Repeat four times.

- Repeat with your left shoulder.

- Do both shoulders simultaneously, release and drop, six times.

## 2b
## Head Alignment and Neck Releasing

- Focus on this thought: your head is lightly balanced, like a large balloon on top of the spinal column (see fig. 2.2).

- Let your head slowly tip backward until it passes the center of balance and then let it drop back as far as it will go.

- Let your lower jaw drop open to facilitate a feeling of completely "letting go."

- Bring your head slowly forward until it again passes the center of balance and then let it drop forward as far as it will go.

*Figure 2.2*

- Let the head float back up to a position where the head (still like a large balloon) feels perfecly balanced on top of the spine. The crown of your head should be the high point.

- Keep the feeling of lightness while speaking [ɑ][1] in a downward sigh.

- Repeat six times, alternating between [ɑ] and [o].

## 2c
## Neck Releasing

- Take a firm hold of your right trapezius muscle with the thumb and index finger of the left hand (see fig. 2.3).

- Slowly turn your head to the right as far as you can, and look over your right shoulder.

- Allow the head to return to center and then repeat this motion five times, turning the head as far as it will comfortably go.

*Figure 2.3*

- Repeat to the opposite side.

- Think or say, "let go" to your body as you are moving your head. The impulse to "let go" must come from within. Let go in the mind first, and then the muscles will "let go."

## 2d
## Torso Releasing and Alignment

- Put your arms over your head and stretch upward.

- While lowering your arms to your sides, hum in a descending sigh. Let the rib cage remain buoyant and the sternum comfortably high.

- Repeat the stretch, and this time let the hum open into an [ɑ] as the arms lower.

- Allow the ears to align over the shoulders. The back of the neck is long, the front of the neck is short and relaxed.

- This is a good way to find the right balanced posture for singing.

## 2e
## Torso Releasing

- Gently rotate your torso from side to side, allowing your relaxed, floppy arms to swing out slightly from your body as a result of your turning.

- Do a lip buzz[2] beginning on a low pitch in the spoken area and ascend to as high as is comfortable and then come back down.

- Repeat the lip buzz, still gently turning the upper body with relaxed shoulders and arms.

- Repeat the downward sigh this time as a hum.

- Repeat the hum.

## 2f
## Vocal Mechanism Releasing

- Massage your shoulders and neck (or have someone do it for you).

- Find the muscular attachment between jawbone and skull (slightly in front of the ears) and massage with fingertips in a circular motion.

- Gently take hold of your larynx with thumb and index finger. Move it gently from side to side while keeping a sensation of the breath slowly coming in through an open, free throat.

---

1. For an IPA chart of the symbols used in this book, see p. 161.
2. A lip buzz is made by holding the lips loosely together and passing sufficient airflow through them to cause them to vibrate while vocalizing. This is the same sound that children often use to imitate the sound of a motorboat or car engine. When using the lip buzz as a vocalise, be sure that the jaw is released, not held.

# 3
# Breath Preparation

*"Every inhalation should prepare the throat for singing."*

*"Leave the body in the posture of inhalation while you sing."*

*"Unless there is an obvious problem, I don't start beginning students by teaching them breathing because I want to see what they do naturally. For some students breathing is never an issue because their bodies already know what to do."*

We are born with the natural reflex of breathing. We spend most of our lives breathing on a subconscious level, but we can also choose to exert conscious control over our breathing. If you watch an infant breathe while sleeping, you will notice deep, natural diaphragmatic breathing. As we grow up and our bodies become misaligned and accumulate muscular tension, we often unlearn this deep breathing. Tension in the torso, especially in the abdominal or intercostal muscles, makes it impossible to take a full breath of air. Teachers compound this problem when they tell students that they "don't know how to breathe." Students then add tension on top of tension as they try to make their bodies breathe the "right way."

For the most direct route to undoing incorrect breathing habits, first release muscular tension in the torso by establishing a balanced posture. Second, discover your body's own natural, reflexive breathing. I often ask a student to notice how deeply they breathe when they are totally relaxed before falling asleep and to observe how easily the breath goes in and out while the breath naturally goes low. The following exercise[1] will help you to discover natural, reflexive breathing:

## 3a

- Lie on your back on the floor with a book (about 1 or 2 inches thick) under your head for support.

- Think of lengthening the spine and releasing your neck.

- Imagine yourself melting into the floor.

- Now imagine that you have a hole in each side of the rib cage. Breathe through the holes with the mouth slightly open.

- Release the breath.

- When the breath is gone, wait. Leave your body in limbo until you feel the need for oxygen.

- Let the body's natural reflexes take over to replace the breath. Do not pull the air in. Simply allow the air to replace itself by letting the body function freely and naturally.

- Once again, release the air. Wait without tension with the body in limbo.

- When your body needs oxygen, simply let your reflexes take over and inhale.

- Now allow your body to find its natural breathing cycle. Allow the mind to be a passive observer as the breath goes out, and then back in. Notice the breath flowing to different areas of the body: rib cage, epigastrium/abdominal region, and the small of the back.

- Slowly stand up, maintaining the feeling of release and relaxation.

- Imagine the spine moving upward as it supports the torso.

- Release the inner muscles of your body by allowing the mind to travel through your body, undoing any tensions you find along the way. Begin from the inside of the top of your skull, down through the inside mask of your face, down through your throat, then through your chest. Notice the movement of your breathing as your mind moves down into the stomach, abdomen, and legs. Gently tell any tensions you find to "let go."

Breathing for singing differs from reflexive deep breathing. The singer must usually inhale quickly and then sustain the exhalation throughout the phrase. Inhalation for singing accomplishes two objectives: First, filling the lungs with sufficient air to sustain the entire phrase, and second, preparing the vocal tract for singing. In order to achieve this first objective the singer must keep the torso free from tension. Standing with a balanced posture helps to minimize tension in the torso. As the singer inhales, the rib cage, epigastrium, and back should expand as the intercostal and abdominal muscles release. Following inhalation, the lungs should not feel crowded with air, but comfortably expanded.

## 3b
## To increase your breath capacity:

• Inhale to the count of 8.

• Now hold (in limbo, keeping the muscles relaxed and the throat open) to the count of 4.

• Exhale slowly blowing the air through the mouth to the count of 16.

• Keep the rib cage buoyant and expanded as long as possible.

• If this rhythm is not comfortable try shorter time increments.

The second objective of inhalation for singing is to release and open the entire vocal tract, so it can properly amplify and project a beautiful tone. The act of inhalation for singing should involve a releasing of the jaw and a relaxing of the larynx into a lowered, balanced posture. While inhaling, you should feel the throat release and open all the way down into the chest. While teaching a young baritone the need to prepare the throat for singing each time he inhaled, I asked him to imagine he was drinking from a glass while inhaling. After giving it a try, he declared, "Oh, it's like chugging a beer!"

The throat can only be opened by the inhalation, not by direct muscular effort. Any attempt to hold the larynx down or to open the throat with muscular effort will cause vocal fatigue and stiffness in the tone. When the throat is open, inhalation is silent. A constriction in the throat causes an audible inhalation and therefore should be avoided.

While the jaw and larynx release down, there should be a corresponding lift of the soft palate. Conscious effort to lift the soft palate, however, can lead to excess tension in the jaw and throat. I encourage students instead to think about lifting the top back molars. While this is not really possible to do, the image of lifting the back molars facilitates a gentler lifting of the soft palate, with just the right amount of muscular activity. To encourage the proper lifting of the soft palate I also have students imagine they are about to yawn. The singer should only imitate the beginning of a yawn, however, because a full yawn activates a number of muscles in the throat that would greatly interfere with healthy singing.

Once you have prepared and opened the vocal tract with the inhalation, think about leaving everything in that open position while you sing. The objective is to keep the larynx from rising and the throat from closing or tightening as you sing. The following exercises will train the larynx to release into the proper lowered, balanced posture when inhaling, and remain in that posture without muscular force while singing.

## 3c
## The Imploded "k" Exercise:

- Very gently place the thumb and index finger on either side of the larynx in the groove between the thyroid cartilage and the hyoid bone (see fig. 3.1).

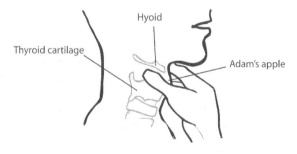

Hyoid

Thyroid cartilage

Adam's apple

*Figure 3.1*

- Inhale on a gently imploded [k] sound. To create the imploded [k], start in a silent "ng" position. Then as you inhale, the tongue drops down, creating a quick, soft [k] sound at the back of the throat. Feel the soft palate lift and the tongue release.

- Feel the larynx release and descend into a lower, balanced position. (You may also feel a slight widening of the space between the thyroid cartilage and the hyoid bone.)

- Speak a vocal glide up and down in a comfortable range on [ɑ], leaving the thumb and finger gently on the larynx to monitor:

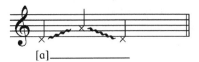

[ɑ]_____

- Observe what the thyroid cartilage does at the onset of tone. If you feel the larynx rise, remind it that it is only the motion of air through the vocal folds, which is required to begin the tone.

- Sing/glide while sending the message to the larynx to stay in the lowered, balanced posture as you begin the tone:

[ɑ]_____

- Modulate up and down the range by half-steps, repeating the steps outlined above.

- Maintain a feeling of floating and balance in the larynx. Avoid trying to hold it in place with muscular effort.

- At first you may not be totally satisfied with the tone as the muscles of the throat get accustomed to a new, more released way of singing. Temporarily turn off any judgments about tone quality and don't worry if the voice feels unsteady. You are teaching the muscles a new way of singing.

- Now sing a five-note scale, modulating up and down the range. Continue to breathe with the imploded [k] in between each repetition:

[ɑ]_____

## Additional Instructions:

- The inhalation on the imploded [k] should involve a feeling of release and openness. Maintain this feeling of release and freedom as you sing.

- As you inhale, think about lifting the top back molars.

- As you inhale, feel the tongue relax forward as the base of the tongue releases. Then as you sing, continue to think about releasing the tongue at its base, letting it fall forward in the mouth.

## Variations:

- Inhale on the imploded [k].

- Speak:

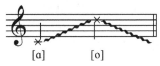

[ɑ]　　　[o]

- Make sure the larynx does not rise significantly as pitch ascends. It should stay in about the same lowered balanced posture throughout the vocal glide.

- A little movement is allowable, since the larynx should never be held muscularly in the lowered position.

- Sing:

[ɑ]_____ [o]_____

- Modulate up and down the range by half-steps, continuing to use the imploded "k" with each inhalation.

## Teaching Tools:

In addition to the above exercises, I also use these images and tools with students:

- Think of the inhalation occurring below the larynx. Notice how this opens the throat and helps the larynx to freely descend.

*Figure 3.2*

- Drop the jaw as if biting an apple. Use a closed fist as your imaginary apple and bring the "apple" up to your mouth, feeling the jaw release, the soft palate lift, and the throat open in preparation to take a bite (see fig. 3.2).

- Prepare the throat by imagining you are "chugging" a drink. This helps to open and release the throat. Maintain that feeling of openness while you sing.

- Think of breathing in, down, and out, while breathing through the nose and mouth simultaneously.

- To prepare with enough breath for a long phrase, pretend that you are about to go underwater to swim a lap in a pool. Notice how when the mind has a clear objective, the body instinctively responds to meet the mind's expectations.

- Imagine filling your back with air as you inhale. One way to help this is to imagine that you have a hole in the middle of your back. Breathe through the hole and leave this imaginary hole open as you sing. This will help the rib cage remain buoyant.

- Bend forward at the waist and place both hands on the lower back. As you inhale, notice how the rib cage expands. Repeat while standing upright.

- Imagine that the back of your neck is opening and releasing as you breathe in. The neck may even feel like it slightly expands during the inhalation.

- Place the hands on the back of the neck with the thumbs gently on either side of the mylohyoid. As you inhale, let the muscles at the nape of the neck feel released and free, and let the head feel light and floating. As you start to sing, keep the released, free sensation. If you have a tendency to tip the head back, you will feel tension at the nape of the neck. The fingers on the back of your neck will help the head and neck remain free and light.

---

1. Adapted from Kristin Linklater's book, *Freeing the Natural Voice*, 26.

# 4
# Breath Management
# and Onset of Tone

*"Many vocal problems may be attributed to lack of breath energy, which leads
to other muscles wanting to take over."*

*"Breath support isn't a lot of effort—it's just the right use of the right muscles."*

*"Don't push with the breath, just energize."*

*"Breathing for singing should not divert from the natural process of breathing
for speaking. It is simply an extension of the natural breathing process."*

*"We should never see a singer breathe, hear a singer breathe, or observe
a singer running out of breath."*

*"Because inherent energy in compressed air secures both pitch and power
of tones, the singer feels the 'control' of breath descend in the body as the
voice ascends the scale or increases in volume. Even soft singing and
diminishing volume of tone demand pelvic control of breath."*
—G.B. Lamperti

Breathing for singing is a synergistic action that involves the coordination of
the diaphragm, the intercostals, and the abdominal muscles. Sometimes
singers develop the mistaken notion that their muscles must behave in an
exaggerated way in order to support the tone. I have worked with singers
who have been taught to pull in, bear down, or push out with the abdominal
muscles at the onset of tone. Inevitably this leads to tension and inefficient
use of the breathing muscles. Singers who try to *make* certain muscles contract at the onset of tone will soon start to think and feel that singing takes a
great deal of effort and concentration, and they will begin to develop habits

of excess muscular activity, leading to a variety of serious vocal problems. A better approach is to discover what it feels like to produce a supported, vibrant tone using what the body instinctively knows about making sound. By relating energized speech to singing or by using natural reflexes such as coughing or laughing, teachers can help students discover an energized and efficient use of breath. Efficiency means achieving the greatest results with the least amount of work. Try the following three exercises to discover a natural and efficient use of the breathing mechanism for singing.

## <u>4a</u>

- Place one hand on the sternum and the other on the lower abdominal area.

- Pretend to cough and notice what happens.

- You should feel an energizing of the abdominal muscles, and a slight thrust of the sternum.

- Now pretend to laugh, but not a fake, half-hearted laugh. Rather, imagine that you just heard or saw something really funny, triggering a hearty laugh.

- Notice again how the body instinctively energizes the tone.

- As you experiment, do not try to make the muscles do what you think they should do. Simply allow the mind to observe the body's natural muscular reflex.

## <u>4b</u>

- Place one hand on the abdomen and the other on the sternum.

- Make a "lip buzz" by blowing air across relaxed lips loosely held together, while also allowing the vocal folds to vibrate. (The resulting sound is similar to that a child makes to imitate a motorboat.)

- Allow the pitch to rise and fall as you do the lip buzz, noticing how the body responds to the changes in pitch.

- Now use the lip buzz to let the voice glide high up in the range then back down again.

- Observe how the body instinctively knows how to give the extra breath energy needed for the higher pitches.

- If you have trouble making the lips buzz, try gently pushing in on the corners of the lips with both index fingers. Resting the tip of the tongue between the lips can also help.

## 4c

- Place your hands on your sides below the rib cage, but above the hip bone.

- Repeat the word "NOW" loudly and with energy as many times as possible on one breath.

- Observe how the muscles are activated by the energized use of the breath.

- Again, do not allow the mind to try to make the muscles do what you think they ought to do. Simply focus on speaking "NOW" with volume and energy and observe what the body does naturally.[1]

This next vocalise is especially helpful for singers who have a habit of working too hard muscularly to support the tone. It helps demonstrate that breath management for singing can feel natural and easy. Lamperti expressed the idea like this, "You cannot sing well, until your least 'hum' excites your whole co-ordination as much as your loudest tone. You cannot sing with your mouth open if you cannot do so with it shut."[2] For this reason, I frequently use this humming exercise as the first vocalise of a voice lesson.

## 4d

[m]          [m]_____

- First do the spoken hum glide. Notice how resonant and easy it feels. Singing is that easy!

- Now hum the descending five-note scale, maintaining the same feeling of ease and resonance.

**Variations:**

[m ɑ]    [m ɑ]_____

[m ɑ m ɑ m ɑ m ɑ m ɑ]

- Allow the hum to open smoothly and directly into the [ɑ] without a break in phonation.

- Allow the [ɑ] to happen just as naturally and as effortlessly as the hum.

- Do not try to manipulate the vowel to sound a certain way. Simply open the mouth and let the vowel emerge.

In some cases, a singer's problem is not over-activity of the breathing mechanism, but *under*-activity. A young lady called me recently to see if I could hear her sing and diagnose what was going wrong with her voice. She sings professionally in the belt and R&B style with a backup group for an award-winning singer. She has had two years of classical training. I first observed that she spoke in a very unsupported way with no breath energy or resonance. When she started to sing I could barely hear her voice, and I was standing only about three feet from her. I had her start again and sing as if she didn't have a microphone. The voice still was very soft and airy. As she progressed and the song went into the higher voice it started to have more ring.

I asked her about her concepts of breath energy and support. She readily explained that she had been taught to always keep the diaphragm high and light "like a balloon." She cupped her hand and raised it as an example of what the diaphragm should do to stay high and light. She possesses a potentially good instrument, but I fear that years of singing without sufficient breath energy has caused vocal damage. I recommended that she see an otolaryngologist, have her cords scoped, and start therapy with a singing vocal specialist, who works to rehabilitate injured voices.

To help singers like this learn to sufficiently energize the breath, have the student make three quick "sh-sh-sh" sounds as if quieting someone down. If done properly, the student will feel the muscular energizing all the way down into the pelvic area.

The visualization of vomiting the tone is another helpful image for singers lacking sufficient breath energy. Most people are familiar with how the abdominal muscles naturally energize and the throat opens when the body needs to remove food from the stomach. When using this image, be certain that the rib cage does not collapse, and that the throat opens completely.

The next three exercises help singers develop a balanced, natural approach to breath management, leading to a free and vibrant tone.

**4e**

- First speak with energy and inflection: "ya ya," then sing. Use the speaking voice as a healthy model for the singing voice. Observe how the breath energizes and the abdominal muscles engage.

- Preceding the [ɑ] with the [j] spontaneously releases the tongue and brightens the [ɑ].

- Modulate throughout the range.

- Go on to one or more of the variations below.

**Variations:**

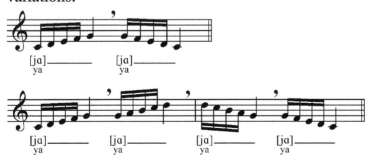

[yɑ o ɑ o ɑ o ɑ o ɑ]

**4f**

[bɑ] [ɑ]_____ [bɑ] [ɑ]_____ [bɑ] [ɑ]_____

- Before singing the exercise, speak "ba-ah" with energy. Place hands at sides below the rib cage to feel the muscular action.

- Allow separation between the [bɑ] and [ɑ] syllables, but be sure to leave the vocal folds open with no glottic stroke before the [ɑ].

- For a variation use [ti] [te] in place of [bɑ] [ɑ].

**4g**

(lip buzz)

- Make a lip buzz by blowing air between the lips loosely held together, causing them to vibrate.

- Keep the rib cage in the position of inhalation.

- Place hands at sides between the bottom rib and the hip bone and feel the muscular energizing that accompanies the onset of tone.

- Go on to the variation below:

(lip buzz)          [ɑ] _____

- Notice how the breath naturally energizes for the lip buzz. Let the breath energize the [ɑ] in the same way.

In summary, after the intake of breath, let the tone activate the muscles of support without consciously tightening the abdominal muscles. At the onset of tone, notice the automatic energizing of the lower abdominal muscles and the area just below the rib cage. A little contraction of the pelvic muscle will give the resistance that is needed to energize the breath. A slight thrust of the sternum also occurs at the onset of tone.

### Achieving a Balanced Onset

A "balanced onset" is achieved when the singing tone begins simply by the motion of energized breath across gently, but fully approximated (touching) vocal folds. A balanced onset helps create a tone that is neither breathy nor forced. The word "attack," formerly used to describe the manner for starting the singing tone, causes a singer to think of a more percussive beginning and should be avoided. Richard Miller encourages the use of "onset of tone" rather than the word "attack."[3] When the vocal folds are allowed to vibrate with the application of the compressed breath there is neither breathiness nor a muscular, glottic sound.

Singers sometimes think that they need to involve the muscles of the throat in starting the tone rather than allowing the tone to begin "on the breath." The Germanic method, for example, teaches "take a breath, get set…SING!" This approach, however, causes the glottis to tightly close before the tone begins. The vocal folds must then be forced apart by a great amount of breath energy, resulting in a glottal stroke and causing undue strain on the vocal folds.

To achieve a balanced onset, each tone must start exactly on the pitch. Scooping the voice up to the pitch sets the vocal mechanism for a lower pitch. In that split second, the vocal mechanism receives the message of the lower pitch and must then adjust to the right pitch. This adjustment is rarely successful and instead results in singing that is too heavy and under pitch. In addition, scooping communicates a feeling of uncertainty that destroys the legato line and shape of the phrase.

A useful tool for achieving a balanced onset is to use an imaginary "h" sound to start the tone. This keeps the glottis open, preventing a glottal stroke at the onset. For singers who habitually begin with a glottal stroke, you may need to use an actual, audible "h" sound for a period of time, until the habit is broken. Then just imagine the "h."

As you work through the exercises below, observe how the singing naturally energizes the muscles of support. No conscious effort is required. When the mind has an objective to make a vocal sound, the body takes over and knows just how much to energize the muscles of support. The spoken [ɑ] and hum in the following exercises help the singer to more fully understand the relationship between the speaking voice and the singing voice (see Chapter 8). I like to use this spoken exercise after the student has felt the ease of the spoken hum in exercise 4d.

**Balanced Onset Exercises:**
**4h**

- First speak [ɑ] three times with inflection. Allow the tone to be easy, natural, and resonant. Remember, a balanced onset begins simply by the motion of energized breath across vocal folds.

- Next sing [ɑ] three times on the same pitch. Allow the tone to be as easy and resonant for the sung pitches as for the spoken.

- Modulate within a comfortable range.

- Avoid beginning and ending the tone with a glottal stroke. If necessary, imagine an "h" sound before the onset of the tone.

**Variation:**

- Allow the pitch changes to occur in a legato fashion, without articulating the individual pitches in the throat.

- Remember to leave the throat in the open posture of inhalation throughout the three-note scale.

The following staccato hum exercises help the singer to feel whether he is using the laryngeal muscles at the onset of the tone rather than starting the tone on the breath. This series of exercises is also a great way to begin a lesson or practice session.

**4i**

[m  m  m  m  m]

- Sing a staccato hum on a single note.

- Place the thumb gently on the soft, fleshy area underneath the chin on the mylohyoid muscle (connects from the chin to the hyoid bone). If you feel the muscle shake or tighten, release the tension by inhaling on an imploded [k] (see Chapter 3, Exercise 3c). Then maintain the released feeling as you sing. This tension will almost always be present if a singer habitually scoops to the tone or starts with a glottic attack.

[m  m  m  m  m  m  m  m  m]

- Sing a five-tone descending scale on a hum. Sing it softly and staccato.

- Breathe in a tiny sip of air between each two notes (at comma markings) to help the rib cage and breathing mechanism stay buoyant.

[m  m  m  m  m]

- Sing an arpeggiated triad on a hum with a short breath between each tone. Sing it softly and staccato.

[m  m  m  m  ɑ]

- Add a legato triad on [ɑ] to the exercise. Strive to maintain the same free-dom of tone on the legato singing as on the staccato singing.

[m    m  m  m  m]
[ɑ    ɑ  ɑ  ɑ  ɑ]

- Sing the hum variation, incorporating staccato and legato singing.

- Repeat the exercise on [ɑ].

[ɑ]

- Repeat the exercise without the staccatos on a legato [ɑ].

## The Technique of *Appoggio*

The Italians use the term *appoggio* to describe the classic Italian approach to breath management which involves a feeling of energy and balance between the muscles of inhalation and exhalation. Proper *appoggio* technique depends on a well-aligned and balanced posture. Throughout the sung phrase, the rib cage or sternum must not collapse. To help a student develop a sense of *appoggio*, I suggest trying to remain in the posture of inhalation as long as possible through the sung phrase. At a workshop years ago I heard the following description of *appoggio:* "The muscles of inhalation are in constant struggle against the muscles of exhalation, and, in singing, the muscles of inhalation must win." In other words, there is a feeling of resistance or energy between the muscles of inhalation and exhalation. The feeling of buoyancy and openness achieved during inhalation, however, must win out over the tendency to compress and collapse during the sung phrase.

Richard Miller defines *appoggio* this way:

*Appoggio* begins as a postural attitude: the sternum must remain at a moderately high, poised position throughout the breath cycle. The sternum finds this position when the arms are raised over the head and then brought down to the sides of the body; at the same time the shoulders are relaxed, making certain the sternum does not lower. In this position the sternum could be raised still higher, but that would be too high; it could also be lowered from this posture by "relaxing" it, which would be too low. This noble posture is perhaps the most visible trademark of the Italian-schooled singer. It is the key to the Italian's breath coordination in singing…Because the muscles of the epigastrium (so often confused with the diaphragm itself) engage the diaphragm, a sensation of internal-external muscular balance takes place during the course of the sung phrase. This feeling of stabilized muscular balance increases with the demands of pitch and power.[4]

Try the following exercises to sense the Italian idea of *appoggio*.

**4j**

[i  i  i  i  e  e  e  e  a  a  a  a  o  o  o  o  u]

- First speak it without pitch, then sing.

- Take a sip of air in between each group of four notes. This helps the breathing muscles to stay buoyant and flexible.

- Make sure that the staccati are articulated with the breath, not with the throat. One way to feel a correct staccato articulation using the breath is to chuckle with closed lips "hm-hm-hm." The motion of the breath, not the opening and closing of the glottis, should cause each tone to begin.

- To feel *appoggio* action in the muscles of breathing and support, try putting one hand on the upper abdomen and the other hand on the sternum. Or place both hands on the waist above the hip bone. Make sure that you keep an outward motion, not a squeezing inward action of the muscles at the sides.

- Modulate in a comfortable range.

- This exercise also helps the singer achieve a balanced onset.

**4k**

[i]— [i]— [e]— [e]—   [i]— [i]— [e]— [e]—   [i]

- Take a small sip of air through the nose by closing the lips in between each set of two eighth notes. Each sniff opens the throat, preparing it for singing. It also keeps the upper lungs inflated and the rib cage buoyant.

Mastering the concept of *appoggio* is crucial for improving the legato line (sense of evenness of tone), vibrato, and phonation throughout the sung phrase. Try the following exercises to help with legato line.

**Teaching Tools:**

- Sing a specific passage of music from your repertoire using the syllables "ri-di-di" in place of the usual text. Sing with lyricism and sense of legato. Then sing the same passage with only the vowel sounds, leaving out all the consonants. Then sing it with a lip buzz. Finally, sing the passage with words, while maintaining the same sense of legato.

- Imagine that you are a string instrument and your breath is the bow. The bow must keep moving on the string in order to make a beautiful tone, just as the energized breath must keep flowing to make a beautiful singing tone.

- When singing, think of bowing to the end of the phrase. Keep the breath moving through the very last note of the phrase, all the way into the next inhalation. This image helps prevent the diaphragm and the costal muscles from becoming rigid or locked.

- With arms outstretched in front of your face, put your fingers together and slowly draw your hands toward your open mouth while inhaling. Repeat while singing a long phrase. This gives the impression that the breath is returning to you. Notice how the rib cage stays buoyant and the throat feels more open and free.

## *Sutherland and Horne on Breath Control:*

Joan Sutherland: *You make your chest cavity as large as possible—and hold it. You breathe only with your diaphragm. Your chest and shoulders never move. You feel as though you're holding up this long column of air on which the voice is resting—like one of these balls on a fountain.*

Marilyn Horne: *And you get these terrific muscles in the diaphragm and in the back—and in the derriere. Really. When I'm singing pianissimo and very controlled coloratura, I feel I've got everything under me...not to mention your legs may be planted like an athlete's. But that is what it takes to hold and measure out that air—let the perfect amount of air gradually pass over the vocal cords—the perfect amount so that the tone is just the way you want it. And I feel almost like the reserve of air goes clear around me like a tire. Maybe that's why we all have spare tires.*[5]

---

1. Adapted from McKinney's *The Diagnosis and Correction of Vocal Problems.*
2. Brown, *Vocal Wisdom: Maxims of Giovanni Battista Lamperti,* 25-6.
3. Miller, *The Structure of Singing,* 1.
4. Miller, *Techniques of Singing,* 41-2.
5. Meryman, "A Tour of Two Great Throats," 64-6.

# 5

## Freeing the Vocal Instrument

*"When the voice is free of tension and the vocal mechanism and body
are in proper balance, the tone will become ringing and vibrant,
and the good vocal health of the singer will be a lasting result."*

*"Many singers' tendency is to do too much. They pay too high a price
for the results they achieve."*

*"Perfecting technique means finding a manner of execution
which produces the best results with the least effort."*

—Oren Brown, Discover Your Voice

*"In the tones of a perfect singer there is no evidence of directed effort."*

*"The feeling that your tone is free, borne on its own wings of energy,
is one of the greatest delights of life—because you are its creator."*

—G.B. Lamperti

Excess tension in one area of the body will inevitably spread to neighboring
areas. On the other hand, when a singer frees excess tension in one area of
the body, all neighboring areas benefit, leading to a freer, more beautiful
tone. I use the phrase "excess tension" because healthy singing requires a
highly energized use of the body. A body completely relaxed and free of all
tension cannot produce a beautiful singing tone.

Many singers get into trouble, however, when they believe that their muscles
have to do more work than is necessary, leading both to fatigue and an
unsatisfactory tone. For example, the abdominal muscles must be engaged
and energized for proper *appoggio* breathing and support of the tone, but

some singers take this idea too far by vigorously pulling in and/or consciously tightening the abdominals at the onset of tone. This may create a dramatic and powerful sound, but instead of a buoyant and round tone, the tone will have an unpleasant edge or a brittle quality, and the singer will fatigue too quickly.

One of my students describes so well her experience with this very problem:

> For years, as a young singer and as a college student, I was taught to take a very low, deep breath and then to use breath "support" in the form of abdominal tensing and rigid posture to produce and sustain the tone. I was taught to breathe low enough that the lower torso could be seen expanding, and then the muscles would visually pull in and tighten in "supporting" the tone.

> This resulted in tension throughout my body. At the onset of the breath I would think of supporting the tone, and instinctively my abdominal muscles would pull in, tighten, and gear up. The higher the notes or the louder the dynamic, the more "support" I needed.

> My tone was big, vibrant, heavy, and pushed. The sound wowed fellow students and landed me leads in several university productions. The price, however, was fatigue. I could rarely sing for more than an hour before pitch and accuracy started to suffer. In addition, my voice was stiff and without significant agility—a characteristic I attributed to my voice type.

> Then I learned a new way to breathe, without unnecessary tension and muscular involvement. I discovered that my lack of agility and vocal fatigue actually originated with the breath! Now my thought process at the onset of the breath goes something like this: breathe in, release the muscles, fill my rib cage, feel my back expand, open the vocal tract, measure the phrase, stay buoyant, and sing!

Not only does this student enjoy singing more now, but by freeing the breath her voice is more beautiful, resonant, and warm. She also uses her breath more efficiently and can sing much longer phrases. She once took three or four breaths in the melismatic phrases in "Rejoice Greatly" from Handel's *Messiah*. Now she comfortably sings the entire phrase on one breath.

The *appoggio* action requires the energized use of the abdominal muscles, but these muscles must never become rigid and immobilized by tension. Place a hand on the abdominals to monitor how they are being used. There is no need to consciously tighten the abdominal muscles at the onset of tone. Sometimes excess tension in the epigastrium region (the soft area located directly below the sternum) can lead to an unstable tone. Place the fingers firmly on this area to monitor how these muscles are being used. They must not become rigid or locked. Notice that when the muscles stabilize and do just the right amount of work, the tone also becomes stable.

Using the right muscles for the wrong tasks is another common problem. For example, singers should use the tongue for articulating consonants and shaping the oropharynx in a way that gives definition to vowels. Some singers, however, use tension in the base of the tongue to add extra color to the tone, a task that should belong solely to the various resonating areas. If this habit persists, the singer will have an overly dark (or bright) tone, difficulty in bridging the *passaggio* (the area of the voice where a muscular shift occurs and the voice passes from register to register or changes from one resonance area to the next) and an uneven vibrato. Voice teachers should concern themselves with releasing any form of excess tension throughout the student's body to ensure a free and resonant tone, as well as the singer's vocal health.

The Alexander Technique helps the singer to free unwanted muscle tension through mental awareness and control (see Chapter 16). Alexander maintained that if you can learn to inhibit your habitual responses, remarkable changes can be made relatively quickly and easily. Otherwise, trying to overlay a new response on top of the old one produces conflict. We have all become so accustomed to our usual way of doing things that it "feels right" to us. Any other way of doing things, even when more efficient, is bound to feel wrong at first.

Muscles have a memory. Teachers can talk a lot about correct technique, but the singer's muscles must actually feel, and gradually over time, habitualize what it is like to sing with proper technique. If one sings with excess tension, then the body must experience the correct way repeatedly over a significant period of time in order to replace the old habit with the new.

Consider this example: a teacher can verbally remind a student to "relax the jaw!" But a much faster and more efficient way to help a student learn to release the jaw is to provide a kinesthetic experience of what it *feels* like when the jaw is released. Inserting a cork between the back molars, for example, gives the student this kind of kinesthetic experience. Do not bite down on the cork, but simply allow the cork to serve as reminder for the

*Figure 5.1*

jaw to release. This teaches the mind what the jaw should feel like while singing. After a sufficient amount of time, the singer may remove the cork, but the memory of that feeling will remain. A singer can call upon that memory during practice or performance. You can purchase corks of various sizes in small and large packages at most craft stores. I prefer the 5/8 by 7/8" size. The smallest I use is a 3/8 by 1/2" cork (see fig. 5.1). For some students I may even use a larger cork, depending on the space between the back molars in the individual student. I most often have the student place the cork upright between the back molars, but sometimes I'll have them turn it sideways for the more closed vowels, such as [i]. After the student uses the cork, send it home with him to practice with throughout the week.

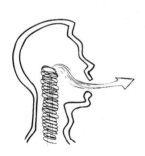

*Figure 5.2*

One of the first concepts I like to instill in a student is to sing freely, letting the voice fill the entire resonating area (see fig. 5.2). I ask the student to visualize an open tube that begins just below the larynx and goes up between the ears as far as there is space. When the resonant tube is open and the muscles of the throat are released the tone will fill the space. The lower resonating area adds warmth to the top and the higher resonating area adds brightness to the lower voice. I also ask the singer to think of the voice beginning over the breath chamber (the spot where you feel the cool air go down as you inhale) spinning on the breath in this resonating tube.

I also use the imploded "k" to help the student feel the vocal tract open and the larynx drop into a lowered, balanced posture (see Exercise 3c). The hum glides help the student feel the natural and easy onset of tone (see Exercise 4d). If there is a problem with excessive motion of the larynx (such as raising when pitch ascends or shaking), try lightly placing a finger on the notch of the thyroid cartilage (Adam's apple) simply to monitor the motion. Let the mind tell your body that you want the larynx to stay in a released, balanced posture while singing.

The concept that a singer must keep the tone "constantly forward" pulls the voice out of the resonating tube, by-passing the wonderful back space that causes the warmth and ring. Placing the voice forward causes tongue tension, a raised larynx, and the muscles of the throat to initiate the tone. When the voice is free, the tone automatically goes forward. There is no other place for it to go. Deliberately pushing it forward causes a stridency and edge to the tone. (See Chapter 6 for more detail.)

Caesari said of this forward singing method:

> In an attempt to trace the origin of this truly pernicious method, the conclusion has been reached that it is due in the first instance to the erroneous interpretation of impressions received while listening to the great singers of the past. Hence, perhaps, the Italian adage: *cantare a fior di labbra* (to sing on the edge of the lips). In fact, when listening to a great singer the general impression is that he is singing forward all the time.[1]

When the tone is on the breath and ringing in the singing tube (or sound column, as Caesari calls it) it sounds forward and there is a discernable feeling of vibration or buzz in the lips and teeth. Caesari continues:

> The critics' pronouncement: *"the tone was well forward,"* was raised to the dignity of dictum. Innumerable teachers whose vocal knowledge and experience were patchy, grasped at the phrase as a potential key to true vocal mechanism and inculcated the forward production principle in their pupils. And so the ball was formed, and set rolling. The forward impression is in such cases, merely an effect, a reflection of focused tone, a continuation of the focused sound column.[2]

The often-taught concept of "putting vibrato in every tone" also pulls the voice out of the resonating tube. It causes the tongue to tense and the mylo-hyoid muscle to tighten. It is better to refer to the tone as vibrant rather than asking a student to deliberately make a vibrato in the tone. The right vibrato causes ring and spin in the tone, with no tensing of the mylohyoid muscle or excess movement in the tone such as a bleat or wobble. (See Chapter 12 for more detail.)

The vocalises and teaching tools in this chapter teach the body and mind what it feels like to sing free from unnecessary tension. Once a singer knows how it feels to sing correctly, he can remember it and duplicate it in his own practicing. Simply increasing kinesthetic awareness and training the muscles to do their proper job corrects many vocal problems.

**5a**
**Releasing the jaw:**

[ɑ]_____

• Put the index fingers at the sides of the mouth and press in (see fig. 5.3).

• Leave the tongue forward and free.

• As you modulate upwards, remove the fingers for high notes above the second *passaggio.*[3]

*Figure 5.3*

**5b**

[kɑ  kɑ  kɑ  kɑ  kɑ]
[kɑ  lɑ  kɑ  lɑ  kɑ]

• Place two fingers on the chin. Press in as you inhale.

• The jaw should drop slightly *back*, but *not down*.

- Use the tongue only, (no jaw action) to articulate the consonants. The jaw should remain released.

- This vocalise helps release the jaw by isolating the movement of the tongue and jaw. It teaches the tongue to move independently of the jaw, and trains the jaw that it does not need to help with phonation or articulating certain consonants.

**5c**

[ɑ]

Figure 5.4

- Put the tip of the index finger in back of the front teeth with the nail facing the throat (see fig. 5.4).

- Let the lower part of the finger rest on the chin.

- Let the tongue lie forward and free in the mouth.

- Then sing the five-note descending scale on [ɑ].

**Variation:**

[ɑ]

**Teaching Tools:**

- Visualize more space between the back molars as you inhale.

- Imagine simply taking your jaw off and setting it down on the piano (see fig. 5.5). Now just let it lie there doing nothing while you sing.

Figure 5.5

## 5d
### Releasing the tongue:

[ɑ]_____

- Touch the upper lip with the tip of the tongue (see fig. 5.6) while singing this vocalise.

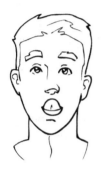

- Drop and release the jaw.

- After a minute or two, return the tongue to its normal position for a few additional repetitions and notice how passive the tongue feels in the floor of the mouth while you sing.

- This vocalise helps the root of the tongue to release.

*Figure 5.6*

- This vocalise is also excellent for training voices to smoothly bridge the *passaggio*.

### Teaching Tools:

- Remember to let the tongue lie lazy in the floor of the mouth.

- Think of the tongue falling forward in the mouth.

- Place a thumb on the soft, fleshy area underneath the chin to monitor the mylohyoid muscle (connects from the chin to the hyoid bone). The mylohyoid should stay loose while singing. Notice when it wants to tighten and simply send it a message to "let go."

- Remember: The floor of the mouth is the cradle of the tongue.

## 5e
## Releasing Tension in the Throat and Larynx:

[ɑ] _____
(vocal fry)

- This vocalise begins with a vocal fry, which is achieved by allowing the relaxed vocal folds to rattle together as air passes between them (similar to how a child would simulate the sound of a large, old, creaky door slowly opening). The throat should feel open and relaxed during the vocal fry. Also, the jaw and tongue should be released and in the right position for the [ɑ] vowel.

- Once the vocal fry is established then simply add enough breath energy to loop the tone up into the normal singing range, followed by a descending five-note scale.

- Make sure the throat does not tighten as you transition from the vocal fry to singing. Leave the throat in the same open and relaxed position, and simply use the added breath energy to create the tone.

- Limit the duration of this exercise, as it can tire the voice.

## Variations (without the vocal fry):

[u] _____

- Speak the vowel on a glide up and down before beginning the exercise.

- Begin with a spoken tone on [u] and glide up to the sung pitch. Then sing down the five-note scale.

[u]          [ɑ] _____

- Repeat the exercise changing to an [ɑ] vowel before descending the scale.

- Sing the exercise on an [i] vowel, and then sing it on [æ].

- This exercise helps lighten a voice with too much weight and smooths out an uneven vibrato.

---

1. Herbert-Caesari, *The Science and Sensations of Vocal Tone,* 168.
2. Ibid.
3. The second *passaggio* refers to the resonance shift from oral to nasal (or middle to head) resonance as the voice goes higher. The second *passaggio* happens at different pitches depending on the voice type. It can also happen at different pitches in the same voice depending on the vowel. See Chapter 10 for a more detailed discussion of registers.

# 6

## Resonance

*"The voice comes forward with enough breath energy.
You don't have to push it forward."*

*"Rather than placing the voice, think of the tone spinning on a column of air."*

*"It is the resonance factor that amplifies the tone. There is no need to push
with the breath—rather, energize the breath."*

*"The process of 'placing' the voice results too often in it being put on the shelf,
where it is indeed useless."*
*—David Ffrangcon-Davies*

*"Tone quality is the first consideration. Never sacrifice it for power."*

*"The perfect tone exists first as a mental concept."*

A singer cannot create a resonant tone by direct effort. Rather, resonance is
the by-product of an open and free vocal tract coupled with sufficient
breath energy. An ideal resonant vocal tone possesses qualities of both
bright (also called "ring" or "singer's formant") and dark (also called
"warmth"). The Italian term used to describe such a tone quality is
*chiaroscuro—chiaro* meaning "light" and *oscuro* meaning "dark." The primary
resonating areas of the vocal tract include the laryngeal pharynx (space in
the throat above the vocal folds), mouth, and nasal cavity.

Ideally, the singer prepares and opens the throat and other resonating areas
with each inhalation. With the inhalation, the base of the tongue and jaw

release, the larynx relaxes down and the soft palate gently lifts. Oren Brown notes the reflexive connection between lifting the soft palate and releasing the larynx: "If the soft palate rises, this assists in creating pharyngeal space and, by reflex action, helps the larynx to rest low."[1] This creates a longer and larger resonating column extending from the vocal folds up to the nasal area. I often refer to this resonating column as "back space." It is important that the act of inhalation, and not direct muscular effort, opens the back space. Any attempt to open the throat by localized effort will engage the "swallowing" muscles and cause the throat to close rather than open. A singer can also use too much muscular force to lift the soft palate.

An optimal resonating column also requires a balanced posture with the ears aligned over the shoulders. The back of the neck should feel long, while the front of the neck is short. To recognize the impact of posture on resonance try this experiment. Stand normally and sustain an [ɑ] vowel on a single pitch in a comfortable range. While continuing to sustain the pitch, jut your head forward, taking the head and neck out of alignment, and notice what happens to the resonance. Bring the head back over the shoulders with the back of the neck long and the front of the neck short, and notice how the resonance returns.

When the singer prepares the back space (resonating column) and uses sufficient breath energy, the tone fills all of the open resonance areas which work synergistically to amplify and project the tone. No conscious effort is needed to produce a forward tone. If the breath energy is sufficient and the vocal tract is properly open, the tone will naturally sound both bright (*chiaro*), and dark (*oscuro*). As long as the singer keeps the back space, he cannot sing too far forward or bright. It is, however, possible to sing too far back or dark. To correct an overly bright or dark sound, we often hear about "placing" the voice forward or back. This notion is dangerous to vocal health, however, because frequently a singer will try to "place" his voice by using tongue tension.

As William Vennard explains,

> The naso-pharynx, and thereby the whole nasal resonator, can be shut off by a sphincter action of the soft palate (also called the *velum*) and the superior constrictor muscle of the pharynx. The part

of the superior constrictor which presses against the velum to produce this closure is called "Passavant's cushion." The cavity itself is
not adjustable, so the control consists entirely of shunting it in or
out of the resonance system. There is considerable dispute as to
which is desirable, or assuming that the passage can be only partly
open, to what extent it should be.[2]

Richard Miller agrees that while complete or partial closure of the velopha-
ryngeal region is debatable, this region does affect the singer's resonance.

> The presence or lack of "resonance" in the singing voice is closely
> tied to adjustments made in the velopharyngeal region (the velum
> and the pharynx). The extent to which the nasal cavities are united
> with the rest of the resonator tube partly determines the perception
> of "resonance." As with the exact character of velopharyngeal clo-
> sure itself, not all the answers are clear regarding the degree to which
> velopharyngeal closure may be modified in singing.[3]

Clifton Ware further clarifies the issue describing how, even though the
extent to which the nasal cavity contributes to resonance is unknown, a
freely produced tone results in unmistakable sensations in the nasal cavities:

> The opening and closing of the "nasal cavity port" is primarily con-
> trolled by sphincter action of the velum (soft palate) and muscles
> connected to the velum. This action determines to a large extent the
> production of certain consonants as well as the tonal configuration
> of vowels. Although the amount of resonance generated by the cou-
> pling of the nasal cavity is questionable, there can be no doubting
> the sensations or illusions of sympathetic resonance vibrations most
> singers experience in the nasal cavities when the tone is freely pro-
> duced. The sinus cavities are small, muted, and practically inaccessi-
> ble due to their small apertures, and therefore are totally unsuitable
> as resonators.
>
> Finally, the coupling of all primary resonation cavities into a single,
> highly complex, and variable resonation system is often referred to
> as the "vocal tract."[4]

One thing is for certain: the soft palate acts as a two-way valve, opening the
pharynx either into the mouth or into the nose. When it relaxes it is in an

intermediate position. I agree with Vennard that the soft palate should be lifted, closing off the nasal port and allowing the tone to have nasal resonance, but not nasality.

When singing with a resonant tone, most people experience sympathetic, or reflected, vibrating sensations in one or more places in their body including the chest, cheekbones, and various parts of the head. While these sensations can indicate the presence of a resonant tone, they are merely a by-product of the tone and do not necessarily contribute to the tone itself. Therefore, while it is good to be aware of these sensations, to directly attempt to make them happen would be potentially harmful, since this will most likely be achieved by adding tension.

In working to develop optimal resonance, singers must remember that how they hear themselves while singing is quite different from the actual sound of their voice. Sometimes beginning singers will shy away from making a fully resonant tone, since to their own ears it sounds too big. Singers need to rely not so much on how the voice sounds as how it feels. They also can and should rely on sound recordings of their own voice as well as the advice and guidance of a qualified voice instructor.

Developing singers should remember not to confuse resonance with power. Resonance can be improved as quickly as a singer can learn to properly open the resonating column and energize with the breath. Power, or the ability to project the voice with great volume and intensity, must be developed gradually over time. The vocal muscles housed in the larynx can only handle so much breath energy from the lungs before becoming overloaded. Their strength and ability to handle greater breath energy are developed over months and years, just as any muscles are gradually built through exercise.

**6a**

[ŋ]    [ɑ]_____

• Drop the jaw as much on the as [ŋ] you need for the [ɑ].

- Be aware of the vibration sensations on the [ŋ] then feel the [ɑ] fill the back space.

**Variation:**

[ŋ   ɑ   ŋ   ɑ   ŋ   ɑ   ŋ   ɑ   ŋ]

**6b**

[m]     [ɑ]_____

- Drop the jaw (like biting an apple) and cover the mouth with the palm of your hand. The covered mouth makes an open hum. Then simply take the hand away for the [ɑ]. Keep the jaw relaxed.

- Be aware of the vibration sensations on the open hum and how the vibrations fill the back of the throat and mouth when the hand is removed.

- Do not push the tone out when the hand is removed; simply *let* the [ɑ] happen as a result of taking the hand away.

**6c**

[ɑ]_____

- Gently press in the corners of the mouth with the index fingers (see fig. 6.1).

- This helps release the tongue and jaw, and automatically creates back space.

- Use this exercise to develop a full, round, and warm tone.

*Figure 6.1*

**6d**

[ɑ] _____

*Figure 6.2*

- Make a fist with one hand and bring it to the mouth while inhaling. Place the upper front teeth on the tip of the middle joint of the fingers keeping the tongue forward and free (see fig. 6.2).

- With the fist to the mouth, sing the five-note descending scale. Begin the exercise in the low part of the range, modulating by half steps as high as is comfortable.

- Observe how the throat opens by reflex action as the fist is brought to the teeth.

**6e**

Bum-ble-bee  Bum-ble-bee  Bum-ble-bee  Bum-ble-bee  Bum-ble-bee  Bum-ble-bee  Bum-ble-bee  Bum-ble-bee

- This exercise helps to open the nasal resonating tube and releases the root of the tongue and the mylohyoid muscle.

- Transpose this exercise up by half steps to practice bridging the *passaggio*.

**Variation:**

- Sing Exercise 6e with two fingers inserted between the front teeth. Try to say the words even though the words will be distorted. Notice the freedom and space created by the insertion of the fingers. Be aware of the nasal resonating area opening as you modulate into the higher voice.

A baritone I was teaching had a very "twangy" and nasal singing tone. He actually loved the feeling of the increased vibration in his nose and resisted my suggestions to add more warmth to the tone. One day, in desperation, I asked him to sing a deliberately nasal tone on an [i] vowel. I then asked him to close his nostrils with his fingers and sing the vowel. This stopped the tone, of course, because it was coming through his nose. Then I had him

sing his normal tone and close his nostrils. It didn't stop the tone completely, but enough that he could feel the air pressure in his nose and mask. Next
I asked him to close his nostrils and sing a deliberately nasal [i] vowel, and
then while still sustaining the [i] vowel, move the sound back to the pharyngeal area. He could feel the soft palate lift as he created the back space.
Then I had him change the vowel to [ɑ]. The resulting tone was amazingly
better. It was now warm and resonant. (He didn't like doing this vocalise,
however, because he said it fogged up his contacts.)

After so many years of teaching, I can seldom remember if I have invented,
borrowed, read about, or stolen a particular vocalise. I know I invented
Exercise 6f in the moment with this baritone. I have since used it with many
other students with much success. Because [i] is a high, forward vowel, the
forward resonance is already established and the student will not sing too far
back. It helps the singer use the entire resonating tube for increased resonance without nasality.

## 6f

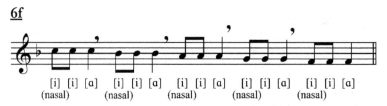

[i] [i] [ɑ]   [i] [i] [ɑ]   [i] [i] [ɑ]   [i] [i] [ɑ]   [i] [i] [ɑ]
(nasal)    (nasal)    (nasal)    (nasal)    (nasal)

- This entire vocalise is performed while completely covering each nostril
  with thumb and forefinger. The first [i] vowel is sung very nasal, which
  should cause a buzzing sensation in the nose. Now add back space while
  still singing the [i] vowel, and notice how the nasality disappears, then
  change the vowel to [ɑ].

- This can be a good way to help singers who have a problem with nasality
  by helping them feel the difference between a lowered and a lifted soft
  palate.

## 6g

[i  ɑ]  [i  ɑ]  [i  ɑ]  [i  ɑ]  [i  ɑ]

- This is a good vocalise for brightening an [ɑ] vowel that lacks ring.

**Variations:**

[i e ɑ]   [i e ɑ]   [i e ɑ]   [i e ɑ]   [i e ɑ]

[i   ɑ   i   ɑ   i   ɑ   i]

In addition to the bright [i] vowel vocalises, for many years I have used the bright, aggressive vowel [æ] to add more brilliance in the classical voice and more of a Broadway sound in the musical theatre voice. The [æ] adds focus, intensity and energy to the tone. Vennard calls it the vowel of anger. "The 'twang' is the most aggressive sound we make. It is the 'bad vowel,' pinched by nasalization." He goes on to warn,

> The work of intensifying the voice must be controlled. It is the part of the medicine that is healthful or lethal depending on the dosage. The student is working for "ping" or "focus," and not beauty of tone. The sound at this stage of the exercise must still be the somewhat unpleasant, neutral, nasal quality with which the exercise was begun.[5]

Vennard also refers to "a synthetic consonant"[6] that precedes the [æ] vowel. When singing the [æ] vocalises, there is indeed a slight glottic stroke that could be described as a "synthetic consonant." For this reason, I add the consonants [kw] before the [æ] vowel.[7] This replaces the "synthetic consonant" or glottic stroke that could quickly tire and potentially damage the voice over time.

The most valuable result of the [kwæ] vocalises is that they help the singer keep the "light mechanism" (cricothyroid) action in the vocal production. Additionally, the jaw drops and releases tension, the thyroid cartilage stays in the lowered balanced posture, and the tongue is free of tension and flat in the floor of the mouth. This results in a production that allows the voice to transition easily from a pop sound to a legitimate classic sound and vice versa. It is becoming increasingly important as teachers of singing to know how to teach our students in a variety of styles from classic, to musical theatre, jazz, pop, rock and belt. I've heard it said, "Bel canto…can belto…can't belto…can't canto." Let us make sure that this does not become the reality for those we teach.

### 6h

[kwæ]    [kwæ] [kwæ] [kwæ] [kwæ]    [kwæ]

- First, "qwack" like a duck or imitate a "baby cry" [kwæ] descending on the spoken sound, starting in the comfortable mid voice. This comes easily, because it is such a natural function, one of the first sounds we make.

- Assure the student that with this exercise, it is OK to make a brassy sound.

- Sing the [kwæ] on a descending five-tone scale.

- Sing it slowly with a breath between each tone.

- In this exercise and the variations below, be sure to modify the [kwæ] vowel with a bright [e] vowel at the second *passaggio*. This vowel modification creates additional space in the vocal column and makes it possible to take the vocalise safely into the high voice. In fact, in some cases it is an excellent way to overcome problems in the second *passaggio*.

### Variations:

[kwæ ɑ] [kwæ ɑ] [kwæ ɑ] [kwæ ɑ] [kwæ ɑ]

- Add an [ɑ] vowel to the exercise with a sip of air between each note. This variation can help brighten a dark [ɑ] vowel.

[kwæ kwæ kwæ kwæ kwæ]
That fat cat is back

- Try this variation of pitches, first on **[kwæ]**, then singing the words, "That fat cat is back."

[kwæ kwæ kwæ]

- Using the **[kwæ]** with the octave jump can help to blend registers, adding more ring to the upper register.

**Teaching Tools:**

To develop a full, round, and warm tone:

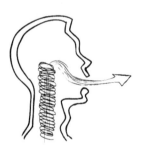

*Figure 6.3*

- Imagine the tone spinning as high as there is space. Visualize it spinning on a column of air (see fig. 6.3).

- Place the hands in front of the ears, palms facing back (see fig. 6.4). Now imagine the tone spinning up behind the hands. The tongue should remain forward and free. This helps open the vocal tract, adding warmth and depth to the tone. Try this with any vocalise or while singing literature.

*Figure 6.4*

- If the [ɑ] vowel lacks warmth, try thinking "awe" with the tongue forward and free instead of "ah."

- Use Exercise 5e (see Chapter 5) to help improve resonance. When singing the vocal fry, be sure to sing the exercise thinking of the correct [ɑ] vowel.

- Use Exercise 5a to create more back space and improve resonance.

To develop a tone with "ring:"

*Figure 6.5*

- Place the hands snugly underneath the cheek bones with the palms facing down (see fig. 6.5). Imagine that the tone is resonating above the hands. Use this to add ring to a tone that is too muffled or throaty. Think: "the roof of the mouth is the floor of the tone."

- If the [ɑ] vowel lacks ring, try alternating [i] with [ɑ] (see Chapter 6, Exercise 6g).

---

1. Brown, *Discover Your Voice*, 80-1.
2. Vennard, *Singing: The Mechanism and the Technic* [sic], 93.
3. Miller, *The Structure of Singing*, 68.
4. Ware, *Adventures in Singing*, 58.
5. Vennard, *Singing: The Mechanism and the Technic* [sic], 218.
6. Ibid., 220.
7. Adapted with permission from Jan Prokop's master class at the University of Utah Voice Disorder Clinic.

# 7
# Diction

*"I sometimes compare the consonants to doorways between rooms, which represent the vowels. You don't spend time in the doorway, but its presence is very important."*
—*Oren Brown,* Discover Your Voice

*"Singing is not just an uninterrupted flow of vowel sound. When you sing, you sing words, which basically alternate vowels and consonants."*
—*Geoffrey G. Forward,* American Diction for Singers

*"Speak the speech, I pray you, as I pronounce it to you, trippingly on tongue, but, if you mouth it, as many of your players do, I would have lief the town crier spoke my lines."*
—*Shakespeare,* Hamlet, *Act 3 Scene 2*

Good diction and articulation are essential elements of beautiful singing. Not only do they make the words and meaning of the song understandable, they aid in building a reliable singing technique. Exercises that use a variety of vowels can be therapeutic to the voice because they require the flexible movement of the tongue and lips as well as a free, open throat whose position and shape determine the vowel sound.

## Vowels
Because the tongue position and tension vary from vowel to vowel, the tongue must remain quite neutral and free in order to shape the vowels. For example, the tongue sits rather flat in the mouth for the [ɑ] vowel, but on the [i] vowel the sides of the tongue touch the inside of the back top molars and tense slightly to shape the [i]. As the singer migrates from the [i] to the [e] vowel the tension lessens and continues to release as the singer moves to the darker back vowels such as [o] and [u].

If the singer tenses the tongue to make a groove or any other shape, the vowel will sound distorted. The tongue must be free to allow the correct shape that each vowel requires to keep its identity. Think of what would happen if you poured unset Jell-O in a wide bowl and then tried to form it in an egg shape as the Jell-O became firm. You would find it impossible, not to mention messy. Now imagine if you poured the unset Jell-O into an egg shaped mold. Without any work on your part, the Jell-O perfectly adheres to the shape of the mold.

In singing, consciously trying to shape each vowel is like trying to shape the Jell-O into the egg shape without a mold. When a singer tries to consciously shape the pharynx in this way, unnecessary tension results and the words sound unnatural and contrived. On the other hand, allowing the body to make subconscious, automatic vowel adjustments is like using a Jell-O mold. The subconscious mind gives the message of the vowel shape to the mouth and tongue, allowing the vowel to form automatically.

It is also possible to shape the vowels and consonants too much. I remember when we were auditioning students at the university for the vocal and choral programs. We could tell nearly every student who went to a particular junior high school because the choral director had her students exaggerate vowel shaping so much that when they came to the university three years later they were still over shaping with their lips and throat, causing tremendous tension in the vocal mechanism.

Conversely, I used to attend concerts at another junior high because some of my grandchildren attended that school. The words of the numbers they sang were muddy and unintelligible. In talking with the choral director after a performance (she was an excellent conductor and had studied with me briefly at the university) she said that she did not like neuter sounds, so she had all of her students modify the schwa vowels to an open "ah," as in "Christmahs."

Another director—who happens to conduct one of my favorite choirs for its artistry and repertoire—has a concept that the jaw needs to be overly dropped to the point that it is hyper-extended. This distorts the singers' vowels creating an unnatural sound, not to mention distorting their facial expressions. Such over shaping of the vowels creates unnecessary tension.

When the pharynx is allowed to freely shape the vowels, a free and ringing tone with unified vowels is produced. As Richard Miller explains, "Unification of vowel timbre results when each vowel is permitted, in freedom, to assume its own distinctive acoustic shape while 'tracking' the frequencies that provide the voice with its carrying power."[1] Exercises 7a, 7b, and 7c help the student feel this automatic adjustment.

## 7a

Choose a column below and let your eyes move down the page, following the underlined vowel as you sing only the vowel sounds on one note. Let one vowel sound flow smoothly to the next. This exercise purposefully occupies the conscious mind with the activity of reading the words, allowing the subconscious mind to make the automatic adjustments for the different vowels. When a singer consciously tries to shape the tongue, lips, and jaw in a certain way for a vowel sound, excess tension results. Notice how this exercise encourages consistent resonance in the tone.

| Dark, back vowels | Mid vowels | Bright, forward vowels |
|---|---|---|
| F<u>a</u>ther | Sof<u>a</u> | Mach<u>i</u>ne |
| P<u>aw</u> | <u>U</u>p | S<u>i</u>t |
| Sc<u>o</u>tch | | Ch<u>a</u>os |
| S<u>o</u>rry | | M<u>e</u>t |
| R<u>o</u>se | | C<u>a</u>t |
| B<u>oo</u>k | | |
| M<u>oo</u>n | | |

- The sequence of sounds for the dark vowels is [ɑɔoʊu]

- The sequence of sounds for the mid vowels is [əʌ]

- The sequence of sounds for the bright vowels is [iɪeɛæ]

Exercise 7b clearly shows the singer how the configuration of the tongue, the soft palate, and—in part—the back wall of the throat shape the vowel. The oral and post-nasal pharynx make up the vowel area, not the mouth or lips, although mouth resonance is also a factor.

Ultimately the singer's goal is to have a free, adjustable pharynx. As Richard Alderson explains:

> The mouth thus becomes more a conduit for the vocal sound rather than a major function in its production, and the vowel formed between the mouth and the pharynx has a better chance to find a harmonic overtone which tunes with the musical pitch. The free method of vowel production depends more on finding natural resonances which fit both the musical pitch and the vowel, rather than forcing the musical pitch into a present combination of resonators or depending on only one resonator to make all the adjustments.[2]

**7b**

[u   o   i   e   ɑ]_____ ____

- For this exercise extend the top teeth over the lower lip. Let the upper lip smile, showing the top teeth (see fig. 7.1). The effect is an exaggerated overbite.

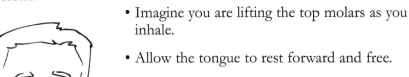

*Figure 7.1*

- Imagine you are lifting the top molars as you inhale.

- Allow the tongue to rest forward and free.

- This exercise helps the student feel how the vowels with the help of the tongue change shape (and resonate) in the pharyngeal area. The over bite holds the larynx in the proper lowered, balanced posture and allows the tongue to assist in vowel formation without tension.

- After many repetitions of the vocalise, try changing to a normal mouth position and notice how easy it is to keep a consistent ring through all five vowels.

Alternating the vowels [i] and [u] helps release the tongue and jaw, letting the mind freely shape the pharynx. The following exercise encourages a balancing of the natural brightness of the [i] with the natural darkness and warmth of the [u] necessary for a good chiaroscuro tone. The two vowels help maintain a balanced tone with a consistent ring and resonant quality.

## 7c

[hʌŋ   n   m   i u i u i u i u]___
"hung"

- Close immediately to the "ng" of "hung."

- Allow the tongue to rest forward and free.

- Be aware of the vibration sensations and maintain consistent resonance throughout.

Also, try these variations.

[hʌŋ   n   m i u i e i u i o i u i ɑ]
"hung"

- This variation helps to balance the five primary vowels. As you repeat notice how a consistent ring emerges and carries through all of the vowels.

[i u i u i u i u i]_____

- Leave the tongue forward and free.


**Vowel Modification**

An entire chapter could be devoted to the subject of vowel modification, but it really can be summed up in a few words: give the vowel a little more space over the second *passaggio*. More specifically, as you ascend the scale and go into the high voice, in the case of the [u] vowel think [o] and in the case of the [i] vowel, think [ɪ]. Since the vowels are formed in the pharynx, the singer does not need to deliberately change the shape of the lips or tongue when modifying the vowel for a high note. Simply thinking of the neighboring, more open vowel, will cause the right configuration for each vowel.

An instinctive or natural singer seems to know just where to add the space in an ascending scale and automatically makes the vowel modification. Again the key is to let the singer's natural instinct dictate just how much vowel modification is needed in each particular circumstance. As stated earlier, the tongue plays a very important role in shaping the vowels and consonants so it must be kept very free to allow it to make quick, subtle adjustments.

For acoustical and physiological reasons, modification of all vowels from their "pure" spoken sound is absolutely necessary in the high voice. Vowel modification adds a certain roundness to the tone. You cannot sing the closed, bright vowels high in the range without giving them more space. The open, warm vowels must also have some modification in the high voice. The exercises at the end of this chapter demonstrate ways to achieve this skill.

**Consonants**

To go into great detail regarding diction for singers is beyond the scope of this chapter. Several excellent books with complete information and exercises have been written on this subject and are listed in the bibliography. However, since singing with understanding and meaning requires good diction, it seems expedient to touch briefly on the correct pronunciation and articulation of consonants.

There are two kinds of consonants: voiceless and voiced. A voiceless consonant uses compressed or flowing air against a resistance of the articulators—the tongue, jaw, lips, teeth, and hard and soft palate—without simultaneous vibration of the vocal folds. A voiced consonant requires both the vibration of the vocal folds and the use of air against or across the articulators.

There is a corresponding use of the speech articulators for each of the following consonant pairs:

| Voiceless | Voiced |
|---|---|
| ch [tʃ] as in **ch**air | dg [ʤ] as in ju**dge** |
| [f] | [v] |
| [k] | [g] |

| | |
|---|---|
| [p] | [b] |
| [s] | [z] |
| sh [ʃ] as in **sh**e | [ʒ] as in plea**s**ure |
| [t] | [d] |
| th [θ] as in **th**in | th [ð] as in **th**ine |

The voiced and voiceless consonants cannot be interchanged or the meaning of the word would be changed: time would become dime, fine would be vine, bray would be pray, etc. Some voiced consonants do not have a corresponding voiceless sound: r, y (as in you), m, n, ng, and l.

The twenty-five consonants can be categorized as follows:[3]

<u>Fricatives</u>
[v] **v**ery, **v**ine
[f] **f**un, **f**in
[θ] **th**e, **th**at
[ð] **th**ank, too**th**
[z] **z**oom, **z**ebra
[s] **s**ail, **s**oda
[ʒ] plea**s**ure, a**z**ure
[ʃ] **sh**out, sa**sh**
[h] **h**ow, **h**ope

<u>Plosives</u>
[b] **b**all, a**b**out
[p] **p**ull, a**pp**le
[d] **d**ear, la**d**
[t] **t**all, lo**t**
[g] **g**ot, do**g**
[k] **c**an, loo**k**

<u>Affricates</u>
[dʒ] **j**ar, fu**dg**e
[tʃ] **ch**air, **ch**urch

<u>Glides</u>
[w] **w**ill, a**w**ake
[hw] **wh**ile, **wh**at
[j] **y**acht, **y**es

<u>Semi-vowels</u>
[l] **l**ake, all
[r] **r**ain, a**r**e

<u>Nasals</u>
[m] **m**an, ca**m**e
[n] **n**ame, ti**n**
[ŋ] so**ng**, you**ng**
[ɲ] o**n**ion

Some singers have the mistaken impression that singing a consonant will break the legato line. When consonants are quickly but distinctly pronounced they enhance the vowel and make the words understandable. Think of the vowel as being like a stream of water and the consonant as a finger passing through the water. It makes an indentation, but does not stop the flow. A critical element in articulation, consonants help focus and project the voice. They are the "doorway" to the vowels.

**Additional Exercises**

**7d**

Fi - glio    a - mor   -    te
Fi - glio    a - mi    -    te

• Use "a-mor-te," "a-mi-te," and "a-mi-a-te" to sense the relationship between the dark and bright vowels.

**Variation:**

Fi - glio  a - mi   -   a   -   te

**7e**

What  shall   I    sing ___ to - day?
I     feel   just  fine ___ to - day!

• Use as a bridge between singing vocal exercises and literature.

**7f**

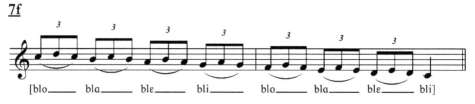

[blo____ bla____ blɛ____ bli____   blo____ bla____ blɛ____ bli]

• This exercise encourages freedom in the tongue, jaw, lips, and vocal mechanism.

• Use this exercise to balance the five vowels.

**7g**

[prɛ  prɛ  prɛ  prɛ   prɛ]

• Use a flipped "r."

- This exercise helps to develop focus in the tone.

**Variation:**

[pri e ɑ]   [pri e ɑ]   [pri e ɑ]   [pri e ɑ]   [pri e ɑ]

- Use a flipped "r."

- Take a sip of air at the comma markings.

1. Miller, *The Structure of Singing,* 74.
2. Alderson, *Complete Handbook of Voice Training,* 128.
3. Forward, *American Diction for Singers,* 150.

# 8
# The Influence of the Speaking
# Voice on Singing

*"The human body is a musical apparatus capable of great precision
and versatility: It can register, remember, implement, and play itself creatively.
But man, so used to using his fingers or his lips or his tongue to play
other instruments, seldom thinks of what he uses to 'play himself.'
He gets along with a note or two—and those often as unpleasant as the
first efforts of an untrained clarinetist—leaving melodies unheard and
rhythms untried. Yet any human voice can range from light, high,
and bright to deep, rich, and dark. It can express sorrow, anger,
melancholy, joy, and so adapt itself to each emotion that it seems
the ideal instrument for each expression. Like any instrument, it must
be played with skill and artistry if its possibilities are to be realized;
yet once you have acquired the skill, you will find it easier to
play well than it was to play badly."*

—*Arthur Lessac,* The Use and Training of the Human Voice

To maintain vocal health it is important that you know your voice both in
speaking and singing. Over the years I have worked with a variety of students with various challenges in their speaking voices. Because of the effect
the speaking voice has on the singing voice—which of course are one and
the same—teachers of singing must analyze how students use their speaking
voice.

One young man, an accomplished pianist who frequently accompanied my
lessons, spoke with a vocal fry in normal conversation. One day when we
had a break I called his attention to the way he was speaking. As we did
some simple spoken exercises he finally got some energy and clarity in his
voice. He said, "Oh, that is what I call my radio announcer's voice." Since
then I have often reminded him to use his "radio announcer's voice" when

he speaks. His habit of speaking with a lazy, vocal fry is so established he will have to constantly remind himself to use his speaking voice more efficiently. The way he speaks is adversely affecting his very nice singing voice.

A young woman came to me recently at the recommendation of her vocal teacher to ask my opinion as to why she was having so much difficulty singing. Her voice tired and her throat hurt after just a few minutes of singing or speaking. An otolaryngologist diagnosed her problem as gastric acid reflux as well as a fungus on her cords. (She did not have insurance and could not afford to have a fiber-optic scope done.) As she spoke to me I could barely hear her because her voice completely lacked energy and resonance. I had her do several spoken exercises as well as a hum. There was no action in her body to suggest that she was energizing the breath. I then had her speak the word "now" repeatedly with whatever energy she could muster. She could only say it five times—singers usually average at least twenty. Next, I had her imagine that she had a sticky feather on her lower lip and asked her to try to blow it off. This caused a little more action in the abdominal and epigastrium muscles, but the intercostal muscles squeezed in and the rib cage collapsed. "Oh, it's my breath that is wrong," she concluded. That was a big part of the problem, but on questioning her further, she told me she thought she was protecting her voice by speaking softly, almost whispering. Actually, she was abusing her voice by not giving any compression or energy to the breath, causing the throat muscles to compensate by tensing. I recommended that she go to a speech therapist and continue with her vocal lessons.

Another student spoke in a very high, "little-girl" voice. If her six-year-old sister answered the phone when I called her home, she sounded older than this seventeen-year-old student. She had quite a mature singing voice when she was in high school, but I was concerned that her speaking voice would affect the development of a secure vocal technique. I recommended that she work with a speech therapist and after just a few sessions her speaking voice had more resonance and depth. She did not achieve this by lowering the pitch of her speaking voice, but by removing tension and adding breath energy.

So often problems with the speaking voice are psychological. It is difficult to know how much the singer's self image influences the speaking voice. There seems to be a trend lately for young women (and some men) on news programs to speak with a nasal, "twangy" tone. Extreme nasality in a speaking voice is far from pleasant to hear. I find it much easier to listen to a warm, resonant tone.

Nothing injures the voice like yelling at a ball game. Even if one does not yell, just talking over the noise of the crowd abuses the voice. Years ago, when I was teaching several high school students, I taught them how to cheer at ball games in their head voices on an [u] vowel. It was quite effective until the referees told them to please not yell that way—it was making it so the players couldn't hear the whistle!

I will not accept a student if they are going to be a cheerleader. It is a waste of time and money for the student, to say nothing of the energy it takes for the teacher to try to counteract the abuse with a weekly lesson. I tell those who audition that if cheerleading is more important to them than singing to call me when they have finished the year and we will see if there is anything left of the voice. I tell them that cheerleading is about as hard on the voice as if they were to chop the piano strings with an ax. A little exaggerated perhaps, but it gives them food for thought.

I have had too many sad experiences with young people who come for therapy after seeing an otolaryngoloist and discovering they have ruined their voices by such abuse. I think of one young singer who had a lovely voice before her cheerleading year. She not only lost her singing voice but also her speaking voice. With speech therapy she regained the use of her speaking voice, but it still remained hoarse and gravely. She became a schoolteacher—a difficult profession for her because she had to use her speaking voice all day long. It was exhausting trying to push past the hoarseness to speak and her voice did not carry.

Anyone who goes into the singing or teaching profession should be required to take a speech class as part of their education. Not only will they learn more about their own voice, how it functions, and how to protect it from abuse, they will learn of the first symptoms of vocal problems in their students. Individuals belonging to any profession that requires regular use of the voice—such as lawyers, actors, politicians, clergymen, or even salesmen—can also benefit from a speech class.

When using the speaking voice we must speak in the optimum pitch level (OPL) that is natural for each individual voice. If we speak higher or lower than our OPL we are in danger of tiring our voices. There are several ways to find the pitch level. Speak the affirmative "uh-huh," as if agreeing with someone. You will usually speak this at your correct pitch level for speaking. Another way to find your own OPL is to put your hands over your ears and hum in a gliding ascending and descending pattern. You will feel an increase of the vibration and buzz when the pitch level is about where you should be speaking.

In addition to speaking in a well-modulated tone, take care to use good breath energy and resonance. Since singing is a function made by the breath, we are actually like wind instruments both when speaking and singing. For this reason, we must energize the breath.

Along with breath energy and speaking in the OPL, we must also have good diction, which means how clearly we say our words. In using good diction we must pronounce properly as well as articulate and enunciate. As Geoffrey Forward explains, these words are often used interchangeably, but there is a difference in their meaning.[1]

**Pronunciation**

Pronunciation refers to the way you say a word, including the vowels, diphthongs, consonants and the way you stress the syllables. For the word to have meaning, the stress must be on the right syllable. Emphasis is not em*pha*sis, and syllable is not syl*lab*le.

Often a singer who has no problem with syllabic stress when speaking forgets to pronounce with the same correct syllabic stress when singing. To remedy this, first try speaking a line from the music with proper inflection and emotion. Then simply try to sing it the same way. Achieving the right syllabic stress becomes an even greater challenge—though no less important to do correctly—when singing in a foreign language.

**Articulation**

Your articulators are your jaw, lips, tongue, teeth, hard palate, and soft palate. Even though the vowels are formed and resonate in the pharynx, the consonants require the use of these articulators to make speech understandable.

Articulating properly involves muscular activity and must be learned. While learning to talk, children imitate the sounds they hear from their parents and siblings. If parents mumble, their children tend to mumble. If they speak with nasality or a drawl, their children will have the same quality. All of these habits of speech will carry over in one degree or another to singing.

When one of my sons was about age 2 and learning to talk, he had a hard time saying the "k" consonant. He would ask "tan I have a too/ee" meaning "can I have a cookie." I would reply, "You may when you say 'cookie.'" I would then work with him to show him how and where the [k] is articulated. He worked so hard that after several tries, I would give him the cookie. He also had a difficult time with the [r] consonant. It took time, practice, and patience, but he eventually got the right feeling.

### Enunciation
Enunciation also involves how clearly you say the words. Each vowel has a particular phoneme (the smallest units of sound in a specified language that distinguish one word from another) made by the configuration of the tongue and shaping of the pharyngeal area. The vowels have different colors produced by different adjustments of the resonators. The articulators create the consonants and must not interfere with the flow of the vowel. When you pass your finger quickly through a stream of water, it makes an indentation for a split second, but the flow does not stop. Consonants work the same way within the context of vowels and legato line. They are the sounds that make speech intelligible.

A healthy singing voice is really an extension of a healthy speaking voice. You can find a correct speaking voice by discovering your optimum pitch level; applying correct articulation and enunciation; using good energized breath; freeing yourself from tension in the throat, tongue, and jaw; and allowing the voice to resonate. This not only results in a healthier voice, but a voice that will project, be understood, and be interesting to hear.

---

1. Forward, *American Diction for Singers,* 1-3.

# 9
# Classification and Range

*"When we free the voice, the range simply grows."*

Classifying young voices is very difficult and very important. It is not possible to classify a voice until a correct technique is accomplished. This takes time and the young singer is usually involved in school, church, or community choirs, where because of limited time the choral director decides which part the student should sing after a very brief audition. Often if a young woman can read music and hear parts she is placed in the alto section regardless of where she is most comfortable vocally. The same is true of the young baritone who has easy access into the high voice: he is often asked to sing tenor. It is very tiring to sing a song where the *tessitura* (the area where the majority of the notes lie in the vocal line) is outside of your comfortable range.

McKinney explains the important relationship between good technique, range, and voice classification:

> When correct techniques of posture, breathing, phonation, resonation, and articulation have become established in the comfortable area, the true quality of the voice will emerge and the upper and lower limits of the range can be explored safely. Only then can a tentative classification be arrived at, and it may need to be adjusted as the voice continues developing.[1]

As the correct technique is established and the voice becomes more mature, it finds its own color. Voices are properly classified according to color and where the *passaggi* occur, rather than range. Many mezzo-sopranos sing as high as lyric sopranos, and in turn many sopranos have wonderful low voices.

It is the color of the tone and where the color change takes place in the range that determines the *Fach* (the German term for voice classification).[2] I do not like to classify a voice, especially a young voice, until I have become well acquainted with the range, timbre (color), and *passaggi*. The mezzo-soprano's *passaggi* usually lie around a major second to a minor third lower than the soprano's, as does the baritone's than the tenor's.

I particularly remember two singers whose lessons bordered each other's when they first started studying with me. One had been singing for years as a mezzo, and the other thought she was a soprano. After several years of study, the student who was singing as a mezzo won the Merola program. I had always thought that she was really a big lyric soprano, but at that time she was in a local opera training program as a mezzo, so I had no choice but to let her keep singing the mezzo roles that she had been assigned. Before she left for San Francisco I had begun to give her crossover arias to change her repertoire. After about two weeks at Merola she called and said, "I don't sound like the other mezzos who are here." I responded by saying, "That is because you are a soprano."

After Merola she performed the role of Susanna in *Le Nozze di Figaro* abroad. When she returned, her lesson again bordered the same student who used to sing soprano and was now singing mezzo. She commented to the new mezzo, "You didn't sound that way when I last heard you." She then sang for the mezzo who responded by saying that she didn't sound like the voice she remembered either!

These changes happened because in freeing their voices the natural vocal color began to appear. The range of the voice has little to do with classifying the voice. The optimum pitch level for the speaking voices of the two singers from the story are very close—they both speak with a warm, resonant quality. Both singers still have the same wide range. The soprano is now singing Verdi roles professionally and sings an E6 above C6 and still has a rich, warm low voice to an F3. The mezzo still has a C#6 and a more resonant low voice to F3. She has performed professionally in oratorio and opera. Even with nearly the same range, there is no question that they are in the right *Fach*.

I have seen the same change of *Fach* for several male voices with whom I have worked. One singer had been asked to sing "The Trumpet Shall Sound" from Handel's *Messiah*. As we worked together, I soon could see that he was really a tenor. I had suspected this because of the texture and color of his speaking voice. The *tessitura* of this aria is rather high for a bass, so the high sections were easy for him. Although he could sing the lower notes, the rich, sonorous color was not there. Even so, he sang very well in the performance. He continued working and is now singing tenor in a professional choir.

McKinney says:

> There are several criteria which teachers of singing traditionally have applied in determining voice classification, but not one of them has gained widespread acceptance to the exclusion of the others. This would seem to indicate that the best approach is a composite one in which all available data are considered. The most frequently applied criteria would seem to be 1) range, 2) *tessitura*, 3) timbre, 4) and transition points (breaks or lifts).[3]

I would change the sequence (in order of importance) to 1) timbre (quality, color), 2) *tessitura* (most comfortable singing area of the voice), 3) transition points, and 4) range. I don't put range first, because frequently a young singer is tightening the vocal mechanism as they go into the higher voice, limiting the range. When they learn to sing properly, with an open throat and sufficient breath energy, the range automatically grows in the low and high areas. I consider the timbre of the voice first and foremost of importance when classifying the voice. You can tell by the quality and the color of the tone whether a voice is a mezzo or a soprano, or a tenor or a baritone.

Establishing a free, flowing voice is more important than increasing range. In addition, as a solid, healthy technique is established in the middle area of the voice, the high and low voice are also influenced and enhanced. I worked with one soprano whose middle voice had a hard edge to it due to a raised larynx from middle C to the octave above (C5). For several months we worked primarily on freeing the vocal mechanism through the middle voice with little attention given to the upper register. After six months of consistent practice and success, the singer brought Manon's "Gavotte" to her lesson, a piece she had studied and performed prior to studying with me. She had always had trouble with the D6 at the end of both the A and B sections, but upon returning to the piece she discovered the notes were now easy, free, and consistent. With no emphasis given to improving the upper register but by simply freeing the middle voice, her high voice improved dramatically.

Joan Sutherland: *You know I never sang the upper B until I was about 18. I always thought that the high C was the ultimate, absolute ultimate. For years I thought I was a mezzo-soprano—and finally it was this husband of mine who heard me just singing around the house and said, "You're crazy because you've got those high notes. You're just scared to use them." He had me stand away from the piano where I couldn't see what notes he was actually playing. And once on a good day, I felt the voice going high and I felt good and he said, "You've got it. You've got it." And I sang a high F sharp…And I've sung very few of those since.*

Marilyn Horne: *That's very interesting. I never knew that. We really are the Bobbsey twins. I never sang low until I was 16—and now the chest register with me is just a natural gift. For me it just comes out—like throwing up. Good imagery? This is something I'd like to know. When you've been in your head for quite a while, how do you come back down and keep a glossy tone in the middle voice?*

Joan Sutherland: *Honey, just don't push it. Let it take care of itself. Be satisfied with the size of the sound you can make. But will we? No, we won't—not with that big orchestra playing away. And you always have this feeling you're walking a tightrope—with a hundred things to break your concentration…you have to concentrate on your voice production, you have a character to portray…I've lost my place so many times it's not news. I mean, we're only human. And your voice really is something that has to be born in one. The manufactured voices aren't around very long.[4]*

---

1. McKinney, *The Diagnosis and Correction of Vocal Faults*, 111.
2. The *Fach* method can be problematic in that a young voice is put in a particular category and then often limited to the repertoire and technique for that *Fach*. This can in turn limit the growth and development as the voice matures.
3. McKinney, *The Diagnosis and Correction of Vocal Faults*, 112.
4. Meryman, "A Tour of Two Great Throats," 64-6.

# 10
# Registration

*"The exact cause of registration in the singing voice is unknown.*
*For those who seek specific information to perfect a teaching technique,*
*the confusion of principle and terminology in voice teaching is indeed disappointing."*
—*D. Ralph Appelman,* The Science of Vocal Pedagogy

Modern technology, including the development of the spectograph and videolaryngostroboscope, has given us more precise images of the vocal mechanism and more information about how the mechanism functions while singing than ever before. Science has its limitations, though, as seen in the area of vocal registration. Because it is not possible to photograph the area of the vocal mechanism in question, there is no definitive, visual proof of registration, although an abundance of aural evidence is available. Thus differences of opinion regarding vocal registers remain even among the most respected vocal scientists, otolaryngologists, speech therapists, and teachers of singing.

Manuel Garcia Jr. defined vocal registers according to the distinct quality that distinguishes each register:

> A register is a series of consecutive homogeneous sounds produced by one mechanism differing from another series of sounds equally homogeneous, produced by another mechanism, what ever modification of timber or strength they may offer. Each of the three registers has its own extent and sonority which vary according to the sex of the individual and the nature of the organ.[1]

Where did the term "vocal register" originate? According to Cornelius Reid:

> The expression "vocal register" is a derivative and was originally employed by organists to describe the many changes of quality

caused by setting up different "stop" combinations. When the vocal organs were discovered to be capable of making sounds of diverse qualities, it seemed natural to refer to each group as a vocal "register." Like the organ, the vocal registers appeared to owe their peculiar and distinguishing characteristics to a special type of mechanical action.[2]

A European research team in defining vocal registers agreed with both Reid and Garcia that registers are defined by a similar quality of sound produced by different mechanisms:

> A register within the human vocal scale is a series of sounds of equal quality...To the male singer the primary register change at the upper part of the scale gives a certain vibrating sensation perceptible to the head. To the female the primary register change at the lower part of the scale gives a certain vibratory sensation to the chest. Each area of identical quality depends upon the adjustment of the resonation cavities. Registers are produced by a mechanism that functions in the production of sound.[3]

These quotes illustrate that pedagogues generally agree that a vocal register can be defined as a region of the voice that has a similar quality of sound, and that the involvement of different mechanisms (or muscles) create the variation in sound from one region of the voice to the next. However, consensus generally ends there. Opinions vary widely as to how many registers exist, how to name the various registers, and finally how best to blend the registers.

## One Register, Two Registers, Three Registers, More?

"The number of registers which are said to comprise the singing voice have been variously listed as none, one, two, three, four, five, six, or seven, with some other teachers of singing insisting that each note in the vocal compass should be called a register."[4] With such a wide variety of opinions out there, it is no wonder teachers of singing have a difficult time knowing how to address vocal registers in their teaching!

The two-register theory describes two mechanisms in registration. First, the heavy mechanism is controlled by the cartilage action of the thyroartyenoid muscles. The main function of these muscles is to thicken and shorten the vocal folds. This register is often referred to as the low voice or chest voice. Second, the light mechanism—often referred to as the high voice or head voice—is controlled by the cartilage action of the cricothyroid. These muscles serve to thin and lengthen the vocal folds.

A proponent of the two-register theory, Cornelius Reid strongly advocated it as the singular explanation of vocal registers. "As there are but two muscle groups engaged in bringing the cords into tension, the only tenable position with regard to the number of registers is that there are two."[5] He goes on to name the registers: "Consequently there are two registers, or mechanisms, in all voices, one called the 'falsetto,' and the other the 'chest.'"[6]

The three-register theory builds on the fundamentals of the two-register idea. The theory that every voice is formed of three distinct portions or registers—namely, chest (lowest), medium (middle), and head (highest)—is the most accepted theory. Those like Garcia who support the three-register concept agree on a chest register and a head register, as in the two-register theory, but they add a third register: the middle or mixed voice. In a certain sense I agree with both the two- and three-register theories. Since the middle or "mixed" voice is neither heavy nor light, but a mixture of both, it could be viewed as a separate, third register or as a blend of the low and high registers. It is this mixed voice that proves essential in blending the registers, as we will see later in our discussion.

Departing from the two- and three-register theories, McKinney describes four vocal registers.

> Research has revealed that the vocal cords are capable of producing at least four distinct vibratory forms, although all persons cannot produce all of them...each of these four registers has its own vibratory pattern, its own pitch area (although there is some overlapping) and its own characteristic sound.[7]

He describes the four areas from lowest to highest as 1) the vocal fry, 2) the normal or natural voice or the "modal voice," 3) the falsetto, and 4) the whistle.[8] Not all agree with McKinney that the vocal fry is a register, although the Tibetan Monks use it in their chants. The whistle register of the female voice, akin to the male falsetto, is seldom used except for a special effect or as a means of working to find the extremely high notes in fioratura singing.

In 1983 Harry Hollein presented a report based on the outcome of a study by a committee of physicians, scientists, and voice pedagogues. The four registers defined by the committee, listed here from lowest to highest, look very similar to those defined by McKinney:

> Register 1: The very lowest of registers, probably used only in speaking (old terms: pulse, vocal fry, creak).
>
> Register 2: That low register, which is used by most for speaking and singing (old terms: modal, chest, normal, and heavy).
>
> Register 3: A high register used primarily in singing (old terms: falsetto, light, head).
>
> Register 4: A very high register found in some women and children and particularly relevant to the coloratura soprano (old terms: flute, whistle).[9]

In addition to these four registers, the committee added a sub-category to the second register, which referred to the register in the middle of the frequency range. "Old terms for register 2A would include *head, mid, middle, and upper.*"[10] Thus, in addition to the low and high register, they added what the three-register proponents referred to as mixed or middle voice.

The four-plus register theories described by McKinney and Hollein separate out the vocal fry, falsetto, and whistle tone from the standard head, chest, and middle voices of the two- and three-register theories. Interestingly, some of these terms were once used interchangeably. As Reid points out, "No longer do vocal teachers include the 'head voice' in the same category of sounds as the falsetto, and this misunderstanding is one of the fundamental departures from original Bel Canto procedure."[11]

The terms "falsetto" and "head voice" are not synonymous. Falsetto is the high feminine sound in the male voice and the flageolet or whistle tone in the female voice. Fiber-optic scope photographs of vocal cords show that the falsetto uses only the medial and distal (front and back) part of the cords with a chink in the middle. This lack of total approximation is what causes the lightness and airiness in the tone. Even before it was possible to see pictures of the process, the old masters knew by what their ears told them that a different vibration and approximation of the cords created the falsetto sound. Since we now have scientific proof of the difference in the fundamental vibration between falsetto and the complete voice, it is not logical to think of the head voice as "falsetto."

## Simplifying the Theories

I often find it helpful when working with students to use the concept of resonating areas rather than dividing the voice into registers. This implies a single, unified voice that simply resonates in different areas of the body—mainly the chest, throat, and head—as pitch ascends and descends. When the pitch is low in the range we feel a sympathetic vibration in the chest and the voice resonates more in the laryngeal-pharyngeal area and in the mouth. As pitch ascends, most singers feel a shift in resonance away from the throat and mouth to higher up in the head.

To help the singer feel the change in resonance in the voice, I have him place his hands on both cheeks and hum a descending spoken sound starting very high in his range. I then ask him to analyze where he felt the vibration increase and change from the head, middle, and chest areas as the voice descends. This exercise is a very good way to help a student get a kinesthetic awareness of where the tone resonates.

## "Placing" The Voice

The fact that a singer senses vocal resonance in different regions of the body has led to the common misconception that a singer can actually "place" the voice in certain areas of the body, such as the head or the chest. The terms chest voice and head voice have also added to the confusion. As William Vennard explained, "The commonly used terms, 'chest voice' and 'head voice,'…are highly figurative and belong to an era when people apparently thought that the voice left the larynx and was 'directed' into these regions."[12]

McKinney also discounts the idea, saying, "Since all registers originate in laryngeal function, it is meaningless to speak of registers being produced in the chest or the head. The vibratory sensations which are felt in these areas are resonance phenomena and should be described in terms related to resonance, not to registers."[13]

I agree with Vennard and McKinney. Not only is it physically impossible to "place" the voice in the chest or the head, instructing students to do so can result in unwanted tensions in the vocal mechanism. Using the term resonance areas rather than registers gives the singer the correct mental concept for creating a free, resonant voice from top to bottom.

## Blending the Registers

Whether you agree with the two-, three-, four-, or more-register theory, admitting that registers exist means also admitting that a blending or mixing of registers must occur to create an even scale and avoid the dreaded "break" or "crack." It is training the muscles in the vocal mechanism to give and take that will result in a smooth transition between registers.

Cornelius Reid explained it like this:

> Before a singer will have completed the full scale, a point will have been reached where it becomes difficult to proceed without making a complete mechanical readjustment of the vocal organs. This is the area of the register crossing, and the singer, in order to continue without strain, is obliged to make the necessary readjustment and transfer to a new register…The crossing point…is known as the "break"…Vocal progress is largely determined by the teacher's skill and understanding in developing and uniting the action of these two mechanisms.[14]

Vennard describes the shift from the heavy mechanism (low voice) to the light mechanism (high voice) as a "tug-of-war" in the vocal mechanism:

> As the cricothyroids contract the pitch rises. Because the thyroarytenoids are active in this adjustment the vocal folds do not elongate as rapidly as they would otherwise. The thyroarytenoids are opposing the cricothyroids. In the lowest tones the internal thyroarytenoids are relaxed and flabby (unless maximum volume is desired). As the pitch rises they enter the tug-of-war that the externals are already having with the cricothyroids. The upper limit of this register is reached

when the limit of muscular strength has been reached. Beginners who have discovered no other way to ascend the scale often "crack," that is, the thyroarytenoids give way, allowing the cricothyroids to win the tug-of-war, and an involuntary falsetto is heard. The singer feels pain from the sudden stretching of the vocal ligaments, and embarrassment at the loss of control, and he stops singing, but if he were to continue he would be in light registration.[15]

It is precisely this "tug-of-war" when moving from the heavy mechanism to the light mechanism that requires a blending of registers. In order to achieve a smooth transition from chest resonance into head resonance, the action of the heavy mechanism must gradually give way to the action of the light mechanism. The area of the voice where this kind of muscular shift occurs is called a *passaggio* and refers to the passage from register to register or the changing from one resonance area to the next. The *passaggio* happens at different pitches depending on the voice type. It can also happen at different pitches in the same voice depending on the vowel and volume.

Both male and female voices have a first and a second *passaggio*. The first *passaggio* occurs where the resonance begins to shift from the laryngeal pharynx (throat) to the oral pharynx (mouth) as the voice ascends in pitch and the heavy mechanism begins to give way to the light mechanism. The second *passaggio* refers to the resonance shift from oral to nasal resonance (head) as the voice ascends yet higher.

While teaching at various high school music programs, I heard the same phrase from nearly every young student that came to sing for me: "Oh I can't start there. That's right where my break is." For the sopranos it usually occurred at B4 and resulted from using the heavy mechanism too high in the range.

The *passaggio* should never be referred to as the "break." If the adjustment of the larynx and the muscles of the vocal tract are tight, the cords might feel as if they could break, but to describe it with that term gives an incorrect mental image that could cause imbalance and tension. It is important to always provide positive messages when using mental imagery. I prefer to use the term "shift" or "lift" when discussing the *passaggio*.

Various schools of thought on how to blend the vocal registers exist, and sometimes are just as confusing as the definitions of the registers. Cornelius Reid in his book *Bel Canto* states that you "separate the registers" and then work to bridge the "break" between the chest and falsetto registers.

> Once the registers have been separated the next step is to promote, by means of appropriate exercises, those quality characteristics natural to each register. The "robust" chest register coming from the "breast by strength" must be built up until the normal power level of the individual voice has been reached, after which this solidity must forever be maintained. The falsetto, too, must by strengthened and brought to a comparable intensity level with the chest register. After these conditions have been satisfied, then the registers are ready to be brought together and made to work as a single, coordinate unit.[16]

Reid's theory suggests that he does not consider that the transition into the mixed tone (the bridge between the chest voice and head voice) is necessary, but has the singer stay in the heavy mechanism until it is no longer possible to take this registration higher and then the voice "breaks" as it adjusts into the light mechanism. He also considers volume of primary importance in bridging the *passaggio*, rather than the transition from the thyroarytenoids to the cricothyroids in the vocal mechanism.

My fear in using this approach is that the singer does not learn to use the mixed tone, which is essential for blending the low and high registers into one unified voice. More damage is done to young voices by carrying the heavy mechanism too high than by any other way of singing. This is also the danger of the belt style of singing when the voice is not allowed to use the mixed adjustment as it progresses into the light mechanism. Some belt styles require a high larynx and a "belter's bite" while the classical style (the belting school tellingly calls it "legitimate"), uses a lowered, balanced larynx and a free jaw.

I agree with Hollein and the three-register theory that a mixed voice must be used in transitioning from the heavy mechanism to the light mechanism. It is this mixed voice that allows for a smooth transition from the thyroarytenoids to the cricothyroids as one ascends the scale and vice versa as a singer descends the scale.

A singer can learn to bridge the *passaggi* if he trains the vocal mechanism to stay in a lowered, balanced posture and provides sufficient breath compression and energy to give the tone momentum to soar upward. Bridging the *passaggi* also requires that the singer learn to let go of the thyroarytenoid muscles while engaging the cricothyroid muscles, and vice versa when descending the scale. This will allow the singer to sing evenly through the lift or shift points between resonance areas. This can be done by developing the mixed tone area which will have a combination of the colors of both the heavy and light mechanisms because both the thyroarytenoid and the cricothyroid muscles are working together as one gradually gives way to the other.

There is yet to be a consensus of opinion on the subject of registration, and there probably never will be a complete agreement. We can, however, draw some conclusions. Even though the color and weight of the voice vary in the different registers (resonance areas), the tone should still contain the same unique qualities of each individual voice. When the voice is free with a proper balance of breath energy and a lowered, balanced vocal mechanism, the singer experiences vocal freedom with practically no change of sensation from resonance to resonance.

**Exercises**

Before beginning work in blending the registers, the singer must have the right basics of healthy singing:

• Good posture

• Correct breath preparation

• Management and use of the breath with good energy and without tension

• An open, released throat and a lowered, balanced posture of the larynx

• Proper shaping of vowels, including the migration of the vowel over the *passaggio* areas. It is important to keep the "point" of the tone (focus) in each vowel.

Once the student has begun to master these skills and before beginning the exercises below, I like to start with a spoken, descending hum, then move to a spoken [ɑ] to establish a healthy, balanced onset in a comfortable range (see Exercise 4d, and use a spoken [ɑ] instead of a hum). Then I use the staccato hum exercises (see Exercise 4i including variations). When singing the hum exercises, the singer will experience a definite feeling at the second *passaggio* that the voice needs to make a slight shift or lift to allow the tone to go into the head resonance. If this is difficult, it often helps to whine like a puppy. Somehow, imitating a puppy whine seems to give a better sensation of the higher resonance and release of the throat muscles.

## 10a
### For developing the head voice:

whoo      whoo

- Allow the jaw to drop as low as it can comfortably go without coming off its "hinge" (see fig. 10.1). The jaw should remain in this lowered position throughout the vocalise.

*Figure 10.1*

- Now purse the lips (without raising the jaw) and make a sound like a hoot owl at a soft dynamic level: "whoo."

- Sing the descending five-note scale *sotto voce* (Italian for "under voice," better translated as "half voice," meaning to sing softly). The tone should be soft and flute-like.

- This vocalise develops the use of the light mechanism, and can be especially helpful for voices that are too heavy. It also helps to balance and release the vocal mechanism. The dropped jaw is important because it helps the larynx to stay in the correct lowered, balanced posture. Note that for the sake of this vocalise the jaw position is much lower than normal for an [u] sound.

- Begin the exercise about a third below the second *passaggio* and work up by half-steps.

**Variation:**

- Leave the jaw dropped as far as it will comfortably go. Change only the lips when going between [u] and [ɑ].

- Maintain a soft dynamic level and a flute-like tone.

## 10b

- First speak/sing a glide on [i]. Allow the glide to extend up through the second *passaggio* and back down again.

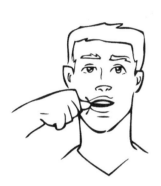

*Figure 10.2*

- Make sure that enough breath energy is used to bridge the *passaggi* without raising the larynx or tightening the muscles of the throat.

- Now sing a five-note scale on [i]. Modulate up by half steps throughout the range.

- Allow the [i] vowel to modify to [ɪ] as you approach the second *passaggio* to prevent the tone from sounding stiff or tight.

- To release the jaw and create more resonance, try inserting the thumb between the back molars with the nail facing the throat (see fig. 10.2).

- This vocalise is helpful for training the voice to make a smooth transition from the heavy mechanism to the light mechanism.

**Variation:**

[i]_____ [e]_____ [ɑ]_____

- One way to encourage more resonance is to make a circle with the thumb and forefinger (see fig. 10.3) and place the circle on the lips (see fig. 10.4) while singing this vocalise. Feel how the back space naturally opens and the jaw releases.

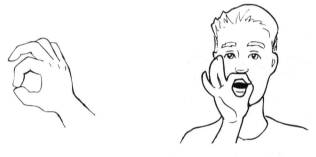

*Figure 10.3*                    *Figure 10.4*

- Exercise 5a (see Chapter 5) also helps the singer bridge the second *passaggio*.

**10c**

It's   ea   -   sy
Ca   -   ro   mio   ben

- Modulate up and down by half steps.

**Variation:**

- Exercise 10a can also help the voice to find the lighter mechanism on high notes.

**For developing the low range:**

**10d**

[mi  si  mi  si  mi]

- First try speaking in a comfortably low, resonant tone: "mi-si-mi-si-mi."

- As you sing, feel the low notes resonating in the same place as for speech.

- Since the high voice needs more breath energy than the low, modal voice, it is important to release the abdominal muscles slightly as the pitch descends.

- You can feel this natural release of the muscles when doing a spoken lip buzz up and down throughout the range.

- If the [i] vowel lacks warmth, have the student slightly round the lips.

**10e**

[lo  a  mo  a  lo  a  mo  a  lo  a]____

- Use this exercise together with Exercise 10d.

**Teaching Tools:**

For singing high notes:

- Try creating more space for the high note by imagining a lift from top molar to molar in an arch shape. This will create a warmer and fuller high note than the common tactic of "spreading" on high notes by pulling back the corners of the mouth, which tends to create an overly bright and shrill tone. Also think of lifting the top jaw more than dropping the bottom jaw.

- To get over the second *passaggio* try a little contraction of the pelvic and sitting muscles. This can supply the necessary breath compression to make a smooth transition from one resonating area to the other.

- As pitch ascends above the second *passaggio*, think about the voice going from the "main floor" into another little attic room, with the vibrations occurring higher in the head, making sure to keep the breath energized.

• Try allowing the voice to shift into the lighter mechanism sooner.

• Sometimes the problem is that the heavy mechanism is carried up too high, and then it is too late for the voice to make the necessary adjustment for a high note.

• Modify the vowel at the second *passaggio* to a more open vowel to create the needed space. Use the migration of the vowel from a more closed to a more open vowel—[o ɑ o], [u o u], and [i–ɪ–i]—to feel the difference through the second *passaggio*. Then work to apply this same concept to the student's literature.

For developing the low range:

• Exercise 5e, which uses the vocal fry, is a valuable way to find the lower mechanism and shows the relationship of the singing voice to the speaking voice.

• Also use the variation of Exercise 5e. Without the vocal fry, speak an ascending [u] and sing down a five-tone scale.

• Repeat on an [i] vowel, keeping the tongue forward and free.

---

1. Manuel Garcia Jr., *Complete School of Singing*, 1847.
   As quoted by Reid, *The Free Voice*, 38.
   As quoted by Appelman, *The Science of Vocal Pedagogy*, 87-88.
2. Reid, *The Free Voice*, 37.
3. Appelman, *The Science of Vocal Pedagogy*, 86.
4. Miller, *Techniques of Singing*, 99.
5. Reid, *The Free Voice*, 40.
6. Ibid., 98.
7. McKinney, *The Diagnosis and Correction of Vocal Faults*, 98.
8. Ibid.
9. Brown, *Discover Your Voice*, 51.
10. Ibid., 52.
11. Reid, *Bel Canto*, 68.
12. Vennard, *Singing: The Mechanism and the Technic* [sic], 66.
13. McKinney, *The Diagnosis and Correction of Vocal Faults*, 98.
14. Reid, *The Free Voice*, 67.
15. Vennard, *Singing: The Mechanism and the Technic* [sic], 66.
16. Reid, *Bel Canto*, 71.

# 11
## Flexibility and Agility

*"It takes more muscle to hold the breath energy back than it does to let it go.
Therefore soft singing is more difficult than loud singing,
and should be studied last."*
—*G.B. Lamperti*

Singers need both flexibility and agility in their singing; both are very necessary for artistic performance. The terms flexibility and agility are confusing because they are often used interchangeably. Flexibility is being able to move from one volume of tone to another with fluent ease that allows for dynamic contrast and tone coloring. This technique is referred to as *messa di voce*. Agility refers to the ability to sing fast melismatic phrases, embellishments and ornamentation such as the trill. These skills must be developed by practicing appropriate vocalises with a completely free functioning vocal mechanism.

## Agility
To sing in different styles and eras of classical vocal music, all voices must be able to sing coloratura. The term refers to embellishments, ornamentation, and melismatic lines, not just the various coloratura soprano *Fachs*. Managing the fast moving passages—such as we find in the music of the Baroque Period and the music of Rossini, Bellini, Donizetti, Mozart, and Haydn—requires the same release of tension in the throat and body as *sostenuto* (sustained) singing. The throat muscles must not articulate the quick movement from note to note in ornamental phrases. The jaw and tongue also need to be released and free. The singer should lighten the voice and think that the larynx is in a floating condition, noting the feeling of increased head resonance.

Oren L. Brown says:

> ...coloratura is so valuable in voice training. The voice moves from note to note quickly, activating new muscle fibers and releasing others. This allows for an exchange of oxygen rather than a build-up of fatigue. At the same time you are exercising a range of impulses that activate many muscle fibers and therefore contribute to their growth and responsiveness. Coloratura conditions reflexive action in the muscles.[1]

I had a student who had been hired to sing an important *Messiah* performance. We had not been working long enough to develop the ability to release her jaw and tongue. To speed things along I had her put a small cork between her back molars. *Voilà!* The melismas and ornamentation became much more consistent and accurate. With just a week until performance, the muscles did not have time for the new memory to hold, so she sang the performance with the cork between her back molars, moving it away with her tongue in the legato phrases. The tenor soloist was so impressed with her performance that he called me to see if I could teach him. The cork simply causes the tongue, jaw, and throat (especially the mylohyoid muscle) to release. It is not a panacea for everyone, but when the need is there, it saves months of trying to get the correct message to the muscles.

**<u>11a</u>**

[i]       [e]       [ɑ]

• Monitor the mylohyoid muscle to see if it is free of tension by putting the thumb under the chin. Be sure that you don't articulate the melismatic notes in your throat.

**<u>11b</u>**

[i]    [ɑ]

- Feel as if you are caressing the notes rather than punching them. Apply the same action of the diaphragm/epigastrium area that you feel on the staccato hum (see Exercise 4i).

### 11c

- There is a feeling of a slight pulse or "toss" of the epigastrium when you sing a correct staccato. The mid-section needs to stay free and flexible.

### 11d

- Extend your arms forward in front of your face, fingers touching. Draw your hands slowly towards your mouth as you sing, imagining the air is returning to you. Do this movement only on the legato portion of the exercise. (See final bullet under Teaching Tools in Chapter 4.)

### 11e

- As with all of the exercises in this section, make sure that you are not articulating the notes with the tongue by placing the thumb on the mylo-hyoid muscle. Be sure that you don't articulate the notes in the throat, and keep the muscles of support free and flexible.

### Messa di Voce

I once heard *messa di voce* described as "the swelling of the voice which makes the music respond to the various passions, and passes the feeling of one mind to another. On it depends the principal art of singing, for it sweetens, enriches, and gives the delicious roundness and fullness to the tone." The *messa di voce* vocalises (not to be confused with *mezza-voce* or half voice) develop a valuable ability, although they should not be used until a secure technique is established.

## 11f

- Begin by singing an [ɑ] vowel with a soft pianissimo. Gradually increase the volume on the same pitch until the full forte is reached, and then slowly diminish the volume to the same pianissimo at which you began. The [i] vowel might work better in some voices.

- After this has been mastered, add:

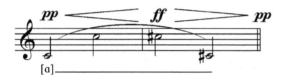

- Modulate up by half steps.

- This rather strenuous exercise must be done carefully. Do not do it to the point of vocal fatigue.

It is best not to use the above vocalises for young voices (ages 16 to about 21) as their voices are not yet vocally mature and their breath control is usually not established. The skill of breath suspension as a component of *appoggio* is necessary to sing a *messa di voce* and since the development of good breath management is always a work in progress, the young singer seldom has this capability because of vocal immaturity. Some gifted young singers (the German term *wunderkind* describes these unusually talented young prodigies), however, are sensitive to expressing music with artistic dynamic variation and capable of doing some *messa di voce*. Even so, I would still not have them do these particular vocalises.

While working for many years with young artists from the Utah Opera ensemble and apprentice training program, I usually asked to hear one of their arias at the first lesson. I could tell immediately if they had the ability to sing expressively and at different dynamic levels or if they plowed through with the same volume and timbre for the entire aria. Even at their high level of singing, many had not yet mastered *messa di voce.*

The *messa di voce* vocalises let singers know what needs to be done to improve their technique and where they stand as skilled singers. More than a technical skill, it enables them to sing artistically. The ability to spin a tone and diminish the volume goes right to the heart of the audience. When a student learns to master this technique I tell them that it will add extra money to their contract.

---

1. Brown, *Discover Your Voice,* 72-3.

# 12
## Vibrancy vs. Vibrato

To be pleasing to the ear, all musical tone must have some vibrato. A musical sound made on any instrument must have freedom and balance in order for the production to allow the natural vibration and fluctuation of the sound. Otherwise, the tone sounds more like a siren. In the case of singing without vibrato, the tone takes on a rather "hooty," thin sound. Acceptable vibrato results from the correct balance between the vocal mechanism and the breath flow and energy.

You prepare the throat for singing each time you inhale. If you inhale correctly, you allow the throat to open all the way down without any constriction of the muscles. The larynx descends slightly and automatically goes into the correct lowered, balanced posture that allows one to sing freely. A quiet intake of the breath ensures that muscle tension has been released. The vocal mechanism that is balanced correctly will produce a beautiful and expressive tone with just the right vibrato rate.

John C. Wilcox describes vibrato as:

> The natural pulsation that is present in every correctly produced tone when sustained at any degree of dynamic intensity beyond the *pianissimo*. The vibrato in a well-produced tone pulsates at a fraction over six per second...This regularly spaced vibrato wave should never be confused with the tremolo, which may be a rapidly waving "bleat" with very small pitch diversion, or a slow uneven "wobble." The "bleat" is due primarily to tension of interfering muscles and the "wobble" to weakness of muscles in the breathing tract and the larynx.[1]

Mozart also disliked the sound of an uneven vibrato. In a letter to his father he wrote, "Meissner, as you know, has a bad habit in that he often intentionally vibrates [he used the term *zittert*] his voice and that I cannot tolerate in him. It is indeed truly detestable, it is singing entirely contrary to nature."[2]

At first glance, it seems as if Mozart preferred a tone without vibrato, but reading further shows that this is not the case. He goes on to say, "The human voice already vibrates of itself, but in such a degree that it is beautiful, that is the nature of the voice. One makes it also not only on wind instruments, but also on string instruments, yes, even on the clavier."[3]

A normal vibrato is inherent in a good voice that is balanced. The assumption that vibrato was invented in the nineteenth century is related to the idea that emotional expression did not come about until the Romantic period. While both concepts are widely held, such ideas insult the humanity of singers of the past and impair the freedom of singers of the present.

Vibrato becomes objectionable when it is irregular, covers too great a range of pitch or intensity, or has a frequency that is too slow or too fast. If the singer can get the concept in his mental ear by becoming aware of the sound and pulsation he can sometimes correct the problem by indirect control (mental imagery and kinesthetic awareness). No vocal problem requires more patience. It simply means that the muscular coordination is out of balance. This can be corrected—not by a few tricks—but by gradually learning a secure technique. When a singer produces his voice as he should, he will have the right vibrato.

Sometimes vibrato problems develop when a singer tries to consciously *make* the vibrato happen. Vibrato problems can also occur when a singer tries to make the tone bigger, brighter, or more powerful. The result of this kind of direct effort is most often a quivering tongue, jaw, or epigastrium region. The vibrato created by such pulsation of one or more components of the vocal mechanism will sound unnatural, will usually be either too fast or slow, and will not be consistent throughout the singer's range. The voice will also tire and strain more quickly because of the excessive muscular activity.

In a *NATS Bulletin* article, John Large and Shigenobu Iwata wrote:

> The vibrato is a modulation of frequency and amplitude result-
> ing from the pendulum like movements of the intrinsic laryn-
> geal level: in other words, the musculature is alternately working
> and resting in vibrato. In the production of straight tone the
> musculature is constantly working.[4]

Remember that a healthy and beautiful vibrato emerges *naturally* in a voice
that is balanced and energized. No conscious effort to make the vibrato happen is necessary. When a singer becomes concerned or worried about the
vibrato, or if a teacher calls too much attention to it, the mind will immediately start to get involved and create problems by adding tension. Vibrato is
a task that must be left to the subconscious mind, rather than the conscious
mind. Because singers can so easily become overly concerned about vibrato,
it is usually best if a teacher does not bring up vibrato as an issue at all.
When a teacher recognizes a problem with vibrato, it is a sign that there is
underlying tension. Rather than asking the student to correct the vibrato
through direct control (using the conscious mind), a teacher should seek to
locate and undo the tension (using appropriate exercises or teaching tools).
Then the vibrato will naturally correct itself.

Singing repertoire that is too difficult or that has the wrong *tessitura* can also
attribute to uneven vibrato and lack of vibrancy. The teacher must carefully
choose proper literature. Songs and arias that stay consistently high (above
the second *passaggio*) or those that stay too long in the lower register, often
result in muscular tension that tires the vocal mechanism. Singing too heavi-
ly and carrying the heavy mechanism (thyroarytenoid) process up through
the mixed voice will also cause problems.

**Teaching Tools:**
*Pulsating tongue*
When the pulsation of the tongue causes a vibrato problem, put the thumb
under the chin on the mylohyoid muscle to physically feel the movement
and pulsation of the muscle. This pulsation, which is also visible, is most
often a result of root-of-the-tongue tension or sublingual tension. The
mylohyoid muscle is tensing and getting involved where it doesn't need to. If
you feel movement and tension in the muscle, that same pulsation will be
evident in the tone.

With the thumb on the mylohyoid, send a message to the muscle to "let go." Sing a descending five-note scale on an [ɑ] vowel. Keep the thumb on the muscle to increase your kinesthetic awareness of what is happening. If you feel tension creeping back in, keep sending the message to the muscle to "let go."

*Shaking epigastrium*
Place a hand on the epigastrium area to discover any shaking that may be interfering with a healthy vibrato. If you feel a pulsation or shaking that corresponds with the vibrato rate, send the message to that area to "let go." Remember that a natural, even vibrato will emerge on its own when the voice is free and properly energized.

*Discovering your natural vibrato*
The acceptable vibrato—the factor heard as the ring and spin of the tone—results from the breath energy, the vibrator (vocal cords), and the resonance system all working together synergistically. Choral directors can encourage a vibrant tone and even vibrato by asking their choirs for a "pure, free tone," rather than asking for a "straight tone." Encouraging singers to sing with a straight tone causes them to tense the musculature of the larynx, the lips, and the tongue, resulting in a tone that lacks vibrancy and ring.

*No vibrato/straight tone*
First, make sure that the throat is opening with each inhalation (use the imploded [k] as in Exercise 3c). After the inhalation, the larynx should remain in a "floating," balanced position. Sometimes a straight tone results from using the throat muscles to hold the larynx in place. With the throat open and the larynx in the lowered, balanced posture, sing Exercise 3c. Rather than trying to make "more vibrato," try thinking of allowing more "vibrancy," "beauty," "ring," or "spin" in the tone. Sometimes simply energizing the tone is all that is needed to encourage the vibrato to emerge.

---

1. Wilcox, *The Living Voice*, 49.
2. Vennard, *Singing: The Mechanism and the Technic* [sic], 207.
3. Ibid.
4. Large and Iwata, "The Significance of Air Flow Modulations in Vocal Vibrato," 44.

# 13
## Interpretation and Expression

Horne: *I was singing Schumann's song* Abendlied *in a recital, and this incredible love of music came over me. I felt this must be what all the music and poetry and beauty in the world is all about. And I just...well, this is why I'm in this game. To be able to experience this one or two times in your life.*

Sutherland: *And I think there's the fact that people really seem to be enthralled by one's singing—in this day when there are so many mechanical means of entertainment. It's that terrible thing of appreciation. But it's not just the applause—though that's fantastic sometimes—this great surge that goes up and up. It's also that letter that one sometimes gets.*

*—"A Tour of Two Great Throats,"*
*by Richard Meryman,* Life

How do singers communicate the mood and feeling of the music they are singing to their audiences? How do they use the words and notes created by the composer and the poet to convey to their listeners the emotion and depth of feeling they have for the music and text? Some highly gifted individuals seem to know intuitively how to shape a phrase or provide a certain nuance to help the meaning come through with the music, but the majority of intelligent students need to constantly work on using the words and notes to reach their listeners with the meaning of the music. Before singers can begin to think about interpretation, they must have mastered a freedom of tonal production so that their voice can respond to the different colors, dynamics, and emotions of the music and words.

In addition to exaggerating and falsely expressing, singers need to avoid lack of expression in both the words and music. Even when the sound is beautiful, a performance without depth of meaning and feeling can be boring and dull. A song or an aria needs that magic touch which comes from the creativity of the performer.

Leonardo da Vinci once said, "The soul desires to dwell in the body."[1] Not only must a singer have the ability to put the soul into his singing, he must use his voice, body, and emotions. The voice must be used with such ease and freedom that the listener is not aware of it as an instrument but rather as a source of beauty expressing an emotional response. One only needs to see a great masterpiece by da Vinci to know what he meant by the soul desiring to dwell in the body. The intangibles that we call soul and spirit become of great importance for the creative spirit of expression.

A singer must become aware and appreciative of the great gift of the five senses. We often find words like "I feel," "I hear," "I see," or "I touch" in the poetry, but do we really hear it, or see it, or touch it? Even more importantly, the singer should ask, "Do I experience anything?"

In performing, however, we must be careful not to get so emotionally involved that it interferes with our vocal production. This does not mean that we avoid feeling the music and message. We just do not allow so much feeling into the performance that we lose control. The expression "all choked up" tells us that emotion is felt first in the throat. When moved to tears the throat collapses and interferes with the delicate balance needed to sing beautifully.

When interpreting it should appear that you have just experienced the thought for the first time. This is sometimes referred to as "the illusion of the first time." This keeps the performance fresh and spontaneous.

The task of getting into the meaning and feeling of a song must take place at the preparatory phase. Study the music and text methodically, creating a subtext (the inner dialogue happening in the mind of an actor or singer) to further understand the meaning of the poem. For example while singing the line, "Sweet chance that led my steps abroad, beyond the town where wild flowers grow,"[2] the subtext could be "I am so grateful to be in this beautiful place at this very moment." Turn an art song into a mini-opera scene and act it out. Think, "What am I expressing" rather than, "How do I sound?"

Singers must use expression through physical movements with naturalness and restraint. Often a singer can give the most powerful expression through the voice alone. In addition, the eyes may mirror the meaning and emotion while the body remains quiet. The hands may be eloquent and expressive in the smallest movement. The head may be lowered and then raised slowly to convey an idea or a mood. These external movements enhance the sincere expression that comes through a beautiful tone in a legato line of ringing, soaring sound.

Lotte Lehmann, considered one of the greatest interpreters of German *Lieder*, said:

> Not only your voice sings—no, you must sing with your whole being—from head to toe…Your eyes sing, your body, animated by the rhythm of the music, sings, your hands sing. How great is the power of expression conveyed by the eyes and the hands! I do not mean that you should never make a gesture which would disturb the frame of concert singing…You should only be in harmony with the song and being in harmony means feeling the unity which is all embracing. Be careful that you do not cultivate the possibilities of expression with the body from the outside, so to speak—I mean by artificial movements—you should learn to *feel* what you are singing with every nerve.[3]

I once heard a tenor make the statement that he thought his high C brought ultimate joy to his audience, when actually, he was so involved with the sound and the mechanics of how he produced it that it said nothing emotionally to his audience. A student once said to me after a master class, "Why is it that Margaret and Naomi each have beautiful voices and I like their singing, but Elizabeth brings me to tears when she sings?" It is that intrinsic thing called "singing from the soul."

**Learning a Song with Expression in Mind**
*1. Study the poem.*
If the poem is in a foreign language, translate it word for word. If you learn

it phonetically without knowing the meaning of each word, you will know the poem as syllables without meaning. Knowing the meaning of each word allows you to give the right inflection and emphasis. Ideally, you should study each language that you sing. When that is not possible, you can learn to sing in foreign languages with authenticity and conviction by coaching with someone who is fluent in the language and who knows the difference between singing and speaking the language. Use the International Phonetic Alphabet (IPA) and listen to recordings of great artists for help with pronunciation. Also see the list of additional excellent sources at the end of this chapter.

Once you know the meaning of every word, analyze the poem's meaning. Read the poem out loud several times with a different interpretation each time. Knowing something about the time period and the country of the composer can also help in interpreting the meaning of the poem.

*2. Write out the poem.*
Writing out the poem separates the text from the music and helps with memorization. Make a sub-text by putting the poem into your own words and weave different images into the words. For example, in Mozart's song "Als Luise die Briefe ihres ungetreuen Liebhabers verbrannte" (As Luise burned the letters of her faithless lover) write of the sad pleasure it gives you to feed his letters to the flames. Write of tearing the pages in pieces and watching them burn. Write of the hurt and sleepless nights he has caused you. Picture the "other woman" who perhaps has been your friend. Ask yourself, "Is it possible that you still love him?" No, and yet you cannot stop thinking about him. You watch as the flames destroy the letters, the memories are not as easy to erase. See how the music turns icy cold as Luise faces a lonely, unhappy future. The flame and pain that he kindled within you will burn for a long, long time. Use the physical action of tearing each page of the letters as you feed them to the flames while speaking the sub-text. Do this in rehearsal only, of course, and not in public performance.

*3. Learn the rhythm and melody.*
Next, analyze the rhythm of the music. Tap the steady beat with one hand and the rhythm of the melody with the other. Then read the poem in the rhythm of the music.

Now you are ready to hear the melody. Play just the melody line on the piano until you have a good idea of it. Try singing the melody first with a lip buzz. I once had a student who had to learn an entire opera role very quickly, so she learned the role in this way. It was actually restful to the voice. Her eyes followed the words while the melody was getting into her head and ear with the lip buzz.

Be sure to learn the notes and rhythms accurately. Unlearning and relearning is time consuming and frustrating. Someone once said when something is learned incorrectly it must be repeated 500 hundred times correctly to erase the old way. George Shirley made the following statement at a master class I attended, "An amateur will practice until he can sing it right. A professional will practice until he can't sing it wrong." As soon as you are sure of the pitches and rhythm, add the phrasing, dynamics, articulation, etc.

*4. Allow ample time for learning the music.*
The voice goes through an awkward stage in every new song. If we allow the ear to learn the music first, involving the voice as little as possible, the vocal mechanism will adapt better. By so doing we can prevent some of the pitfalls of learning new music. One of my mentors said that when we learn a new song or aria we "destroy" the throat, and it is up to the teacher to put it in the throat correctly. This is perhaps a rather exaggerated way of explaining the need for learning music methodically and carefully, but there is some validity to it.

It is better not to "cram" a role or even a song to memory, but sometimes it is necessary. Those few with perfect pitch are more successful at "cramming," but it still takes time to get the music into the voice and memory. Ideally, before performance, a song or a role should be as comfortable as a favorite pair of old shoes.

Listening to a good recording can also aid the singer in getting the notes, rhythm, and accompaniment into his ear. The singer should never copy every nuance of the singer on the recording, but the singer can benefit by listening for good diction, phrasing, dynamics, etc.

*5. Know the background of the music and poem.*

Singers must also know the historical background and the period in which the music and poem were written. Each era—Renaissance, Baroque, Classic, Romantic, or Contemporary—has its own individual style and the music from that era must be sung accordingly. We need to classify the type of song we are studying. Is it an art song, oratorio aria, opera aria, folk song, or spiritual? We must know these things to sing a song in the right style. Style is the individual characteristic by which the compositions of one era differ from the compositions of another era.

*6. Work to express the emotion and meaning of the music.*

Once you have analyzed the poem and the music and thoroughly learned the pitches and rhythms, you can begin to unleash the emotion within you. Albert Schweitzer said, "No more light shines out of you than is in you." How can a singer put feeling into a song or an aria which is not yet in him? The words and notes on the page are at best a pale reflection of the life that inspired them. The singer's contribution is to cause the words and notes to possess real life, to transcend a mere recitation in performance.

Pierre Bernac quoted Gisele Brelet as saying, "Musical performance is not material realization, but rather the spiritual function that this realization exercises."[4] Bernac added, "All the interest of the performance lies in the fact that, to be faithful to the work he performs, the interpreter has to give his personal vision of it. Only the performer's *presence* can give expression to his rendering."[5] Even in audio recordings, the artist's voice must communicate this presence in the expression of the words and the music.

If a singer is too inhibited or is not expressing enough variety of emotion, try the following fun activity inspired by Wesley Balk. First, prepare flash cards with words in large print and faces expressing different emotions. As you or your student sings, hold the cards up one at a time, in random order. Each time a new card is displayed the singer adopts the corresponding emotion. This not only gives the singer some fresh interpretive ideas, it helps them release tension and forget their inhibitions.[6]

Imagination is of great importance if a singer is to develop the ability to portray various roles. The audience wants to believe that the singer is the person they are portraying—Mimì, Carmen, Lohengrin, or des Grieux.

I remember attending a play in which an English friend of mine played the main character. He was so completely the person he was playing that I totally forgot who was playing the role. When I told him the effect it had on me, he responded, "That is the greatest compliment an actor can have."

Singers must not be afraid to act and to use imagination. Even when listening to a single song or aria, an audience can tell if the acting is not honest, is not well thought out, or is contrived. Thus singers should take acting classes to develop and hone their skills. Some have an innate ability to act, while in others the ability lies dormant until it is awakened. Unfortunately, some singers remain very wooden no matter what they do.

Some singers have a certain magnetism or ability to capture the audience emotionally. When an audience feels this magnetism they respond by giving back what they feel to the performer. Each audience has its own personality and brings out different responses from the singer. We have all experienced doing the same program for different audiences where the audience response has varied so greatly that the same music seems completely different. Regardless of the audience response (real or imagined), it is up to the singer to continue giving his very best even if he feels the audience is unresponsive. Giving way to a feeling of insecurity immediately shows in our performance.

I once sang an afternoon program where I could see the faces of the audience. One woman looked as if she was grimacing, and I thought that my singing must be causing the poor woman extreme pain. I tried not to look at her, but my eyes kept returning to her face. At intermission, we happened to be at the drinking fountain at the same time. She said to me, "If I could sing half as beautifully as you, I could die happy." As she said those kind words, she had the same grimace on her face. I then realized that she had a slight facial paralysis that caused the expression.

In addition to not jumping to conclusions about an audience's response, that experience also taught me not to look directly into the faces of the audience, but to keep my eyes just above the heads of the listeners. This gives the appearance of looking at each person, and avoids the possibility of anyone's expression interrupting your focus and concentration.

Not only can you lose your concentration, but if you are looking directly at someone, your eyes cannot show the emotion or mood of the song or aria. Some musical theatre renditions or cabaret type singing are exceptions to this, but as a rule it is best to follow the above advice. Someone once said, "The eyes are the windows of the soul." Let them express your depth of feeling and soul in your singing.

**Additional Excellent Sources to Aid the Singer in Interpretation and Expression:**

- *Phonetic Readings of Songs and Arias* by Berton Coffin, Ralph Errolle, Werner Singer, and Pierre Delattre

- *Word By Word Translations of Songs and Arias, Part 1: German and French* by Berton Coffin, Werner Singer, and Pierre Delattre

- *Word-by-Word Translations of Songs and Arias, Part 2: Italian* by Arthur Schoep and Daniel Harris

- *The Penguin Book Of Lieder* by S. S. Prawer

- *The Ring Of Words: An Anthology of Song Texts* by Phillip L. Miller

- *Facets of a Singer's Art* by Weldon Whitlock

- *Masters of the Italian art song: Word-by-Word and Poetic Translations of the Complete Songs for Voice and Piano* by Timothy Levan

- *Complete Opera Libretti* by Nico Castel

- The Lied and Art Songs Text Page at www.recmusic.org/lieder/

- The Aria Database at www.aria-database.com

---

1. Nuland, *Leonardo da Vinci*, 100.
2. Head, "Sweet Chance That Led My Steps Abroad."
3. Lehmann, *More Than Singing: The Interpretation of Song*, 13.
4. Bernac, *The Interpretation of French Song*, 2.
5. Ibid., 3.
6. These cards are available through *Classical Singer* magazine at www.classicalsinger.com.

# 14
## Vocal Health

*"If the human voice is the grandest of all musical instruments,*
*it is indubitably the worst treated."*
—E. Herbert-Caesari, The Voice of the Mind

Singers need to keep their instrument in optimum condition at all times. Many take the vocal instrument for granted and are not even aware of the abuse they put it through in everyday living conditions. All those who work with singers need to emphasize the importance of sufficient rest, good diet, proper exercise, and sensible use of the vocal instrument.

If the vocal health of a student is ever in question, the teacher should immediately refer him to a doctor who specializes in this field. I find it interesting that when something goes wrong with someone's voice, the person often calls a teacher of singing instead of a doctor. It reveals how we take for granted the health—and limits—of our voices. Physical, mental, emotional, and nervous variations affect our voices.

Jean Westerman Gregg said,

> The speech/voice area of the human body includes not only the respiratory (chest, lungs, abdomen), phonatory (larynx), resonatory/articulatory (throat, mouth, nose systems), but also the neurological (cranial and spinal) integrity of all of those systems, to put it in general terms. Looking at it realistically, all of the above systems are essential in order to sustain life. If any of these areas is affected by disease and so is in jeopardy, the human being can be in serious trouble.[1]

For this reason a voice teacher must work closely with an otolaryngologist and speech therapist. Dr. Gregg continues, "If a voice teacher without training in this area were to attempt to 'cure' the vocal problem, valuable time would be lost which might be the difference between life and death for the singer/patient/client."[2]

A year or so ago, a former student called and asked if I would write a letter of recommendation for membership in the National Association of Teachers of Singing. I could tell when she called that she was hoarse, and when she came to pick up the letter her voice sounded even worse. I recommended that she see a doctor as soon as possible. She taught junior high school choir and also dance and exercise classes. She also taught vocal lessons after school and on Saturday. The endoscopic examination of her cords showed that gastric/acid reflux had irritated her vocal cords, and she had nodules.

With medication, rest and careful work with a speech therapist her condition improved. She began voice lessons again, and we worked carefully with voice therapy, including humming and simple vocalises. Her very concerned principal arranged for her to have a microphone in all of her classes. An exuberant, enthusiastic person with loads of energy, she always spoke a little too high and fast. She now speaks at a better optimum pitch level and rate than before. Her singing voice is nearly back to normal with one major difference: her low voice is more resonant and has extended down to a full G3. Before her vocal damage she was a lyric coloratura with a top extension to F7. We haven't worked the extreme high voice yet—time will tell if it is still there.

It is not natural for the voice, when used properly, to get hoarse or strained. The throat should never hurt when singing and if it does you are abusing the vocal mechanism in some way, usually as a result of poor technique and improper training. Vocal rest will temporarily make things feel better but will not solve the problem. If your throat hurts when you sing, it is time to get a second opinion and perhaps seek a new vocal teacher.

First and foremost in maintaining good vocal health, singers need to develop a secure technique. Someone once said, "Technique is the liberator of the soul." It is certainly the liberator of the voice. Hopefully, the contents of this book along with a good teacher will help singers gain a secure, safe technique to ensure a lifelong enjoyment of beautiful singing.

Avoid singing with too much force, singing too long at a time, and singing out of your comfortable tessitura. If your voice feels tired in a choral rehearsal, mouth the words for a while. No one knows how your voice feels but you. If your throat hurts or feels tired, it is time to give it a rest. If you have a cold that is affecting your voice, do not sing at all, especially if you have laryngitis.

I once taught a very talented young high school baritone who came to me with a damaged voice. In response to my questions about how he used his voice, he informed me that he and three of his friends loved to sing together. They sang before school, during class breaks, in the school choirs, and after school. They loved imitating their favorite singing groups, which included everything from barbershop to rock. I sent him to an otolaryngologist who said his vocal cords looked like hamburger. After vocal rest and therapy we started lessons. The muscle memory was so established that I don't think he will ever be the singer he could have been. He was a victim of singing too high, too loud, and too long. Even so he received his bachelor's degree with an emphasis in voice and is now working on his master's degree in business administration.

**Warming Up and Warming Down**
Since singing is an athletic function, it is important to warm up the voice before performing just as an athlete does before a game or competition. Most singers develop their own regime, so find what works best for you. Warming up should begin with physical muscle releasing exercises such as yoga, brain gym, or stretching. Use the Alexander Technique to release tension (see Chapter 16). Begin working in the mid-voice with the humming and spoken vocalises or anything that will allow you to feel a free emission of vocal tone.

It is best not to use the extreme low or high range when warming up. When asked how he warmed up before a performance, a prominent tenor listed exercises that only involved the mid-voice. When asked if he did anything for his high voice, he replied that he only had so many high Cs to sing and he wasn't going to drop them on the dressing room floor. If the mid-voice is warmed and the color is warm and lovely, the high and low voice will be the same.

Singers seldom think to "warm down" their voices after a performance. Massaging the jaw, neck, and shoulder muscles will help. Going through the Alexander Technique of sending the message of release to the body is another beneficial warm down. Also, try speaking and singing on a descending [u] vowel.

As much as the audience enjoys meeting the artists after a performance, talking and greeting people after a strenuous performance is not the best thing for the health of the voice. Ideally, singers should have a bite to eat in a quiet environment and go to bed.

In addition to developing a healthy lifestyle—including proper diet, sufficient sleep, and sensible exercise—it is also important to know that some medications, food, and drink can adversely affect the voice.

## Medications

Many medications are harmful to the voice. Even aspirin causes adverse effects like dryness of the mucous membranes. It also causes swelling of the blood vessels which can lead to hemorrhaging of the vocal folds. Antihistamines, ephedrine, sleeping pills, and diphenhydramine are a few of the over-the-counter (OTC) medications that are extremely drying.

Cortisone should not be used except in emergency situations where cancellation of an important performance is not possible. In some cases, it reduces inflammation of the vocal cords. Cortisone does not cure the ailment, however, and singing in such a condition can cause serious damage to the vocal mechanism. The singer should always consult with his otolaryngogist before taking cortisone. You must obtain a prescription. It is not a good idea to take a few pills you have left over. Sometimes other alternatives suggested by your doctor can be helpful without the risk of damaging the vocal mechanism.

## Allergies

OTC antihistamines cause drying and decrease vocal cord lubrication which leads to irritation and frequent coughing. Seasonal allergies warrant some form of medication, but most OTC remedies have side effects that are sometimes worse than the allergic symptoms. Dr. Anthony Jahn suggests considering stinging nettle capsules as an alternative treatment.[3] Stinging nettle has good anti-allergic effects without causing dryness or drowsiness.

## Hormones

Menstrual cycles, contraceptives, and menopause can all influence a woman's hormone levels and thus affect her voice. Recognizing the correlation is the first step, and there are additional things a woman can do to minimize the effects. In discussing hormones and the menstrual cycle, Dr. Anthony Jahn observed, "Voice changes during the normal menstrual cycle are well known and documented."[4] European opera contracts for women include a clause excusing them from performing on the days of their menstrual cycle. Dr. Jahn continues:

> The voice becomes husky and loses focus, the top notes are impaired, and the singer is fatigued and has difficulty sustaining. These changes are due in part to fluid retention associated with the fluctuation of estrogen and progesterone and are most marked in the progesterone dominated pre-menstrual phase. These changes, caused by hormones secreted by the body, however disconcerting, are temporary, and are due to the effect of these hormones on blood vessels and mucous membrane.[5]

Dr. Jahn also describes the effect of contraceptives on the voice.

> It appears that nearly 80 percent of singers who experienced voice change after oral contraceptives had some permanent change… This…has to do with the chemistry of the synthetic hormones…It may surprise you to know that women form not two, but three sex hormones: estrogen, progesterone, and testosterone. Although we normally think of testosterone as a male hormone, a small quantity is normally formed by the ovaries and has a number of functions, including regulation of sex drive. The fluctuation of hormones during a normal menstrual cycle involves primarily estrogen and progesterone, not testosterone. It has been shown, however, that *synthetic* progesterone-like chemicals, such as are found in oral contraceptives,

break down to form testosterone-like substances. What this means is that, when a singer takes oral contraceptives which contain progestins, she is actually taking a certain amount of testosterone. We know that, unlike the temporary effects of estrogen and progesterone, the darkening and masculinization of the voice brought on by testosterone can be permanent. Unlike the "female" hormones, testosterone acts on cartilage and muscle and thus brings about structural changes in the skeleton of the larynx and its muscles.[6]

A mature woman came to me for advice because she was losing her high voice and found it difficult to sing as she had formerly done with ease. Her speaking voice was hoarse and rather masculine sounding. I recommended that she see an otolaryngologist. An endoscopic examination showed the mucosal wave slightly decreased and a "post chink" in the glottic closure. She had received six androgen injections in the past six months. This was the cause of her problem. Unfortunately, this condition is not reversible, and the damage was permanent.

**Hydration**
In many cases it is necessary to take medications that cause dryness of the mouth and throat. Always drink a lot of water to help counteract the dryness. Singers need to keep hydrated at all times. While directing a workshop, Sherrill Milnes asked for a pitcher of water and glasses for all the singers saying, "Singing is a wet business." At a NATS convention Dr. Van Lawrence closed his lecture with, "Remember to pee pale."

We should keep the humidity of our homes at a good balance. When we heat our homes in cold weather, the air becomes very dry. Use a humidifier to replace the moisture. When traveling, let the shower run for a while in the hotel room to add moisture. The air in airplanes is especially dry and is circulated throughout the plane with the collective bacteria and viruses of all the passengers. If we were wise, we would wear a surgical mask as many do in Asia. When traveling by air, drink water frequently to stay hydrated. Keep a moist cloth to your nose, or even better, use a personal humidifier. Talking over the noise of the plane can also tire the voice. Take a good book and tell your companion that you prefer to read rather than talk while in flight.

## Smoking

It is inconceivable that a singer would choose to smoke, and yet some do. In addition to being terrible for your health, smoking causes drying of the vocal cords and larynx, eliminating the natural lubrication created by the body. It can damage the epithelium which must function properly to allow free vibration of the vocal cords. Its effect on the lungs shortens breath capacity and increases the risk of lung cancer. The residue left on the laryngeal and bronchial tubes is irritating and causes coughing. Fortunately, at least in the United States, smoking is not as prevalent as in former years. Secondhand smoke wreaks as much havoc on the vocal tract as if you were actually smoking. Thankfully many airports provide smoking rooms, and most airlines do not allow smoking on the plane.

## Drinking Alcohol

Alcohol and other drugs, even those prescribed by a doctor, dry out the vocal cords and larynx, reducing the natural, instinctive reaction of the vocal mechanism. Oren Brown adds, "Alcohol relaxes muscles and swells the mucous lining in the throat. One's ability to monitor the voice is greatly reduced. A single cocktail will affect the voice for five hours."[7] Liquid cough syrups and medications often contain alcohol. Always check the labels.

## Environment

Fumes from paint or chemical products such as turpentine irritate the vocal mechanism. Air pollution also irritates the voice. Some regions have "bad air days" where the elderly and asthmatics are advised to stay indoors and wood fires are prohibited. If you enjoy a wood fire, be sure to add humidity to the room.

## Food

Your singing voice depends on your physical stamina which comes from energy in food. The foods you eat and how you treat your body greatly influence how much energy you have. The body and mind are the singer's instrument. Since your body is your instrument, take special care to keep vitally healthy by living a sensible lifestyle.

Singers should not eat just before they sing. A good balanced meal should be eaten about two hours before a performance. Avoid milk, cheese, yogurt, excessive salt, orange juice, tea, coffee, chocolate, and ice cream. Some singers like to drink tea with lemon before a performance or at intermission. Tea and lemons contain tannic acid, however, and when used in combination really dry out the throat. Caffeine causes gastric reflux and dryness. Avoid junk food the whole day of the performance. Because of the high carbohydrate count, it takes more energy for the body to digest the junk food and causes you to feel bloated and tired.

If you suspect that you have gastric reflux, check with your doctor (preferably an otolaryngologist) and tell him of your symptoms. Symptoms include heartburn, constant hoarseness, a feeling of needing to clear your throat, and/or a sensation of burning just below the larynx. Several medications can relieve the symptoms of gastric reflux. Adjusting your diet and not eating before going to bed, however, are the most helpful remedies.

Consider these tips for gastric reflux relief:

• Have no food or water three hours before retiring to bed.

• Wear loose pajamas.

• Elevate the head of your bed by propping it up on bricks.

• Avoid foods that promote reflux:

  -Caffeine

  -Milk (drink only 1 percent)

  -Peppermint

  -Coffee

  -Alcohol

  -Tea with lemon

  -Chocolate

  -Citrus fruits

  -Any foods with high acid content

## Care of the Voice After a Tonsillectomy

A tonsillectomy is major surgery and a singer must know what to do before, during, and after the surgery. Be sure to let your surgeon and anesthesiologist know that you are a singer. If the operation is performed with intubation, it is imperative that the tube is properly lubricated. Talk with your surgeon before the operation about the removal of the tube. He must remove it slowly. If it is jerked out, the epithelium sometimes adheres to the tubing, and this can seriously injure the vocal folds. This causes hoarseness or even a loss of speaking or singing ability.

Ask your laryngologist's advice about the use of the voice while you are recovering and when to start carefully vocalizing. I recommend waiting for ten days before you start trying to use your voice. Begin with a gentle spoken "hum," for only about five minutes at a time twice a day. Increase the time to ten minutes after the second or third day. Next sing an [ŋ] on a descending five-tone scale. Then do the [ŋ-ɑ] variations of Exercise 6a (Chapter 6).

All of these should be done in the normal, middle range. Do not try to sing in the high voice at this stage. The soft palate area must be flexible before you attempt to sing in the high voice. If you have a tickle in your throat, stop singing and wait a few hours before trying again. When you haven't used any muscle for a while, it will feel a bit weak and you may have a little tingle as the circulation begins to flow. The throat is the same. When a singer has not been singing for a period of time, it will take awhile for the musculature to regain complete coordination.

The scabbing over of the wounds happens the fourth and fifth days after the surgery and can cause a great deal of discomfort as scar tissue forms. At this time, you must be particularly careful as any stretching of this area could cause hemorrhaging. After the healing is complete, stretch this area by gently pulling up on the muscles where the tonsils were (the pillars of the throat or the fauces). Stretch one side at a time. This will help the soft palate area to become more flexible and prevent the fauces from shortening as they heal.

Make sure to ask the surgeon if he intends to remove the adenoids. One of my students had the unfortunate experience of needing a second surgery to remove them because they were diseased and enlarged. The turbinates commonly cover the adenoids and prevent them from being seen.

Above all, give yourself time to heal. In addition to your throat, your body must have time to regain its strength before you get back to your regular routine of physical exercise and everyday activity. The body must be strong before it can manage the breath for singing. If the breath is not energized the muscles of the throat will want to compensate. Start singing for short periods of time, gradually increasing the time as strength permits.

**Therapy Exercises**

The following exercises are helpful when working with a student recovering from the irritation caused by Gastroesophageal Reflux Disease (GERD) or after vocal rest for recovery from nodules.

1. Take hold of your larynx with your thumb and forefinger. Gently move it from side to side while slowly inhaling through the mouth and nose as you move it back and forth.

2. Release your neck as you inhale. Mentally tell the nape and the back of the neck to release and expand as you take your breath.

3. Massage your jaw (the masseter muscles) in a rotating movement. Hum on a descending glide downward and upward as you gently massage your jaw.

4. Do a lip buzz upward and downward. This may also be done with the tongue between the lips or with a tongue trill.

5. Speak on a descending glide on a hum. Then sing a descending five-tone scale keeping the ease and feeling of the hum.

6. Put your fingers gently on either side of your larynx. Inhale on an imploded [k]. Feel the larynx go a little lower and release tension. Speak an [ɑ] vowel on a glide from C5 to F#5, then sing a five-tone scale keeping the same release of the throat and mylohyoid muscle (the muscle under the chin) that you feel on the spoken glide. (See Exercise 3c.)

7. Put your hands on your sides just below the rib cage, inhale through your nose and throat, feel the rib cage go outward. As you inhale, all of the muscles of the upper and lower torso should have a feeling of release.

8. Now, imagine that you have a sticky feather on your lower lip. Try to blow it off in short puffs. Feel the contraction of the lower abdominal muscles and observe that there is also a slight thrust of the sternum. The next breath occurs with the release of the pelvic and lower abdominal muscles.

1. Gregg, "On the ASHA-NATS Joint Statement," 49.
2. Ibid.
3. Jahn, "Seasonal Allergies," 16.
4. Jahn, "Vocal Health," 14.
5. Ibid.
6. Ibid.
7. Brown, *Discover Your Voice*, 231.

# 15
# The Dynamics of the Changing Voice

*"The first teacher is the most important teacher."*

*"With all of the disheartening descriptions of the 'aging voice' it looks like the only remedy is not to grow old. As difficult as it is to grow old, the alternative is less desirable!"*

Singing teachers work with voices at every level of vocal development. From the prepubescent voice, to the adolescent changing voice, to the aging voice, the voice undergoes a myriad of changes throughout a lifetime. Understanding the voice at each stage of development is critical.

## The Young Voice

In Zoltán Kodály's home country of Hungary, as in most European countries, music is an integral part of the school curriculum from elementary through high school. Children have the advantage of not only learning the fundamentals of music and rhythm, but they are exposed to singing on a daily basis. This early exposure instills in them a positive mental image that singing is as natural as speaking.

I like the following statement attributed to Kodály: "Only when it is based on singing does a musical culture develop…The human voice, the finest of all instruments, free and accessible to everyone, can become the fertile soil for a general musical culture."

I believe that Kodály is speaking of the education of children, not just the gifted. Those who are born with an instinctive desire to sing, have been gifted with a lovely singing tone and can sing a melody on pitch, are indeed fortunate, but music and singing should be made available to all children.

In an Alexander Technique based study, Ron Murdock learned that if children were given tone matching games the coordination between the ear and the larynx was developed and children that had been "droners" learned to match pitch and sing in tune. In his four years of teaching music in schools to children between ages 6 and 13, not one of hundreds of children he worked with were unable to match pitch. It took about three months of one half-hour lesson per week of tone matching exercises before they could all sing in tune.[1]

One of my grandsons and his little boy, who had just turned seven, dropped by one day to see me just as I had finished teaching. I told him the young lady who was leaving had come for a singing lesson. His response was, "I already know how to sing." Indeed, he does. He has the sweetest, purest voice. He attends a private school where music is still a part of daily classes and thus sings a lot at school, in addition to at home and in church. His father tried to explain the difference between just singing and learning to sing so you could make a CD, be on television, or in an opera. We didn't carry it too far because I didn't want him to think that singing was something that had to be learned for fear it would take away the spontaneity of his singing.

Why are so many children reluctant to sing? It is largely because they have not had the opportunity. The most important thing we can do for the young singer is to instill a desire to sing. With music being eliminated from the elementary school curriculum, if children don't sing at home or in a church setting they grow up without experiencing the joy of singing. The only music that they hear are the CDs of rock groups and whatever is offered on programs they watch on television. This kind of "singing" is more like yelling and does not give an example of beautiful, fun singing. Sometimes I wonder how the good use of the singing voice and appreciation for beautiful music will survive.

Over the last two decades the trend in music has been towards rock and belting out the voice. This has influenced the way most elementary children sing, not only at school but also at home and church. Children used to sing in their head voices and by doing so learned to sing freely and easily. However, with the trend towards using the belting voice, the vocal mechanism becomes so out of balance that the throat tightens and does not adjust properly as their voices go into the higher range. The larynx rises with the pitch instead of staying in a comfortable lowered and balanced posture.

In his book *Discover Your Voice*, Oren Brown says,

> I want to repeat that, in training children's voices, no attempt should be made to have them sing loudly or for too long at one time. Singing should be fun. It should be a happy experience of discovering different parts of the voice. The pressure placed on children to achieve goals beyond their years very often comes from ambitious parents. In that case, the parents should be invited to attend the lessons and learn what a child's voice is capable of doing. I once attended an audition of children's voices for a radio program. One little girl sang with a pushed and squeezed quality that sounded like no one else. The director of the program immediately gave special attention because her voice was so distinctive. When I spoke to him about the danger to her vocal health because of the way she was singing, he replied that he didn't care about that because the quality would get attention on his program. He said that if her voice gave out, he would find someone else.[2]

Many young people ruin their voices by singing "belt" style roles such as Annie. Famed throat specialist Chevalier Jackson said,

> About 95 percent of promising young voices that start out on a career fail because the laryngeal phonatory mechanism will not stand the long, grueling ordeal of vocal training. Though a faulty method may be ruinous, voices can be forever ruined by excessive singing by any method. Prevention is better than cure. Laryngeal muscles must have rest.[3]

When my young students are not progressing properly, I question them about their singing habits. I often find that they are singing along with the popular recording artists. Their radios and recordings are playing constantly in the car or at home, and they sing along not knowing the damage they are doing to their voices as they imitate the various singers in a variety of poorly produced sounds. After a few years of singing with records and car radios, the wrong adjustment of the vocal mechanism is already established before the teacher can get the right message to them.

Singing is an art that requires time, patience, and skill. Vocal freedom and control must be properly established at a young age to enable the student to sing effectively in later years. Teachers cannot do the work alone. Students must learn to bear the responsibility of learning how to use their voice properly through study and practice. If the throat hurts while singing, something is not right. They need to seek help from their director or find a good teacher of singing. The throat should never hurt while singing.

## 15a

- Teach adolescents to sing in their head voice to extend the upper range.

- Have them speak a light [u] vowel on a descending glide and then sing an octave descending scale (see Exercise 10a, Chapter 10).

- Some will feel their voice go "thump" as it migrates out of the head, but if they keep using the vocalise properly, they will gradually be able to smooth out the transition.

### The Changing Adolescent Male Voice

To sing or not to sing—that is the question for the changing adolescent male voice. In spite of the many research studies that have been done over the years, there are still widely differing opinions on whether or not the young male should sing while his voice is in the process of changing. Most junior high choral directors work very successfully with the young singers in their classes, girls and boys alike. Girls' voices also go through a maturing process, only not as noticeable as with the young men. Just as you can tell the difference between the speaking voice of a little girl and a young woman, the same difference exists in the singing voice.

The majority of educators, laryngologists, speech pathologists, vocal teachers, and researchers have in recent years been on the side that both boys and girls can sing safely through adolescence. It is the absence of competent guidance for young voices that presents the greatest problem. It is even more difficult for the choral directors to teach their young choir members how to use their voices with a lovely, free sound when they have so few good examples of beautiful singing.

Unchanged male and female voices are basically the same. Young men should continue to use their voices during the changing process. In most cases they can sing safely from G3 to G4. The important thing is how the voice is used. Follow the rule of not singing too long, too loud, or too high.

## The Maturing Voice

Individual voices mature at different ages. Some have mature sounding voices when they are in their early teens, while other voices do not develop until early college age. Vocal maturation is a constant, gradual process, which peaks sometime between the ages of about 25 continuing to between the ages of 45 and 55.

Some wonderful young voices are sounding mature at younger ages. This often results from creating a darker vocal tone by stiffening the tongue and holding the larynx down. They think that singing with that kind of tension sounds more mature and operatic. It might even give an increased sense of control, but the muscular control used in place of singing on the breath leads to vocal damage. Young singers who use this kind of technique will shortly develop a wobble and definite breaks at the first and second *passaggi*.

I once had an 11-year-old girl come to audition for lessons. The family was very musical and played a lot of opera recordings in their home. This young lady fell in love with opera and started imitating the singers she heard. I normally do not work with a voice so young, however I accepted this young singer because she would have ruined her voice if she had gone on imitating the mature voices she listened to. She needed to learn how to protect her voice from strain and abuse as well as how to sing safely and correctly.

My first advice to this young woman was to stop singing with recordings and to only sing the repertoire that I gave her. We started with early Italian art songs. These did not satisfy her artistically so we moved on to the more romantic songs of Donaudy. The voice was mature sounding and had lovely ring and warmth. She was also physically maturing very early and at age 12 she looked more like 16. No matter how she looked and sounded, she was still only 12. Once in a while I would let her sing "O, mio babbino caro" or "Vedrai carino," even though she wanted to sing "Vissi d'arte" and "Un bel di vedremo." I found it difficult to choose repertoire that I felt was safe because she was in demand as a performer. Teachers must carefully guide ambitious, young singers to repertoire appropriate for their age that encourages healthy vocal production.

## Late Bloomers

At the other end of the spectrum are those who desperately want to pursue a singing career, but are late in vocal development. Even when they are musically talented it is difficult to know how they are going to progress until they have reached a certain level of vocal maturity. When the late bloomers audition for the university music programs, they are sometimes not accepted as performance majors. It is not fair to have them go through the expense and hard work of four years majoring in music when it is likely they will not succeed as career singers. It is like giving them a road map to a blind alley. Yet if in their heart and soul they want to be singers, they should be encouraged to develop their talent by studying privately and taking music classes.

A young lady at the tender age of 18 applied to the university where I was teaching. Although she was very expressive and musical, her voice was very immature, thin, and breathy. She was not accepted to the music program and was encouraged to go into music education. She started studying with a teaching assistant. She auditioned each year, and even though she had improved she still was not accepted as a major. I started teaching her when she was a junior, and even as a senior she was still not accepted into the program. She came back as a graduate student, majoring in musicology. The second year of her master's studies she sang the role of Rosalinda in *Die Fledermaus* with great success. The following year she entered the Metropolitan Opera Auditions and was one of three who advanced to the region.

Her determination and hard work paid off. In spite of the many rejections she kept working towards her goal to be a singer. As a result she has enjoyed many years of rewarding singing. She married a wonderful pianist and now they both sing with the local opera company. Their two children often take children's roles in some of the productions. With such rejection, not many young people would have had the tenacity to stay with their goals and work hard enough to realize success. If we had been negative and discouraging because of her slow to mature voice this story might have had a different ending.

## The Aging Voice

The symptoms of aging vary from person to person, just as they do in the maturing process. Much depends on the health of the person as well as how the voice has been used. Diseases which affect the connective tissues, such as lupus, osteoporosis, and even arthritis, have an effect on the voice. Medications can also cause vocal problems (see Chapter 14).

Dr. Robert Thayer Sataloff states:

> Normal aging affects all segments of the voice-producing mechanism. Abdominal and general muscular tone frequently decreases, lungs lose elasticity, the thorax loses its distensibility, the mucosa of the vocal tract atrophies and the mucous secretions change character, nerve endings are reduced in number and psychoneurologic functions differ. Moreover, the larynx itself loses muscle tone and bulk and may show depletion of submucosal ground substance in the vocal cord. The laryngeal cartilages ossify and the joints may become arthritic and stiff. The hormonal environment changes. Vocal range, intensity, and quality all may be modified. Atrophic vocal cord changes may be the most striking alteration. The effects of the changes of aging seem to be more pronounced in female singers. Excellent male singers occasionally extend their careers into their seventies. However, some degree of breathiness and other aging changes should be expected in most elderly patients.[4]

Vocal teachers often have older people come to them for an evaluation or advice. They complain that they can't sing like they used to. In many cases it is from disuse, while in some it is misuse or abuse. Depending on the physical condition of the vocal cords, if they begin exercising the voice every day with the right voice strengthening exercises the voice can be rehabilitated. It takes a lot of patience and diligent practice focused on the purpose of each vocalise.

One older woman in her seventies came to me for an evaluation of her voice. She was a voice teacher and needed to keep the ability to sing. For several months her voice had been making a sort of double tone especially in the first *passaggio* area. After working for several months without much result, I suggested that she have her cords scoped by a doctor. The diagnosis was that the vocal cords were bowed which kept them from closing and vibrating in the normal undulating way. Since there was no vocal abuse or misuse the doctor diagnosed her condition as being caused by osteoporosis and arthritis. This condition progressively worsened so the doctor recommended a surgical procedure to inject fat from her own body into the cords. This was done, but without any improvement. A few months later, the doctor repeated the process but still with no improvement. Ongoing research regarding various injection and surgical procedures will hopefully improve the results of such operations. The singing voice needs such delicate balance and fine tuning. It will be interesting to see if the various surgical procedures available can actually restore a singing voice.

Nothing lasts forever. Just as our knees, eyes, ears, and other functions do not work as they used to, we sometimes must realize that our singing days are over and we should be grateful for the time that singing blessed our lives. Many singers sing into their seventies and even eighties. In discussing several singers who had careers for more than thirty years Oren Brown says, "Proper exercise has been shown to deter the deterioration of bodily functions that traditionally accompany aging."[5]

The same holds true of the singing instrument. Brown goes on to tell of Hugues Cuenod, the Swiss tenor, who made his Met debut at age 87. (Incidentally, Cuenod celebrated his 105th birthday in 2007.) Roland Hayes was still giving recitals in his eighties.

> These examples demonstrate that when you use your voice correctly, provided that you have good health, you can sing for years…You know the saying: "Use it or lose it." Singers with long careers keep their voices in condition by vocalizing regularly. This is especially important with respect to the upper half of the voice, which is not used in ordinary conversation. A daily routine of light exercises is a must.[6]

Dr. Robert Sataloff explains it this way,

> Singing is an athletic activity and requires good conditioning and coordinated interaction of numerous physical functions. Maladies of any part of the body may be reflected in the voice. Failure to exercise to maintain good abdominal muscle tone and respiratory endurance is particularly harmful in that deficiencies in these areas undermine the power source of the singing voice. Singers generally will attempt to compensate for such weaknesses by using inappropriate muscle groups, particularly in the neck, that result in vocal dysfunction. Similar problems may occur in the well-conditioned vocalist in states of fatigue. These are compounded by mucosal changes that accompany excessively long hours of hard work. Such problems may be seen even in the best singers shortly before important performances in the height of the concert season.[7]

To maintain good vocal health and sing well into your later years, you must carefully exercise the voice each day. You are the only one who can protect your voice. Only you know how the voice feels. If the throat is tired or hurts in any way, do not sing; it is a sign that something is not right. Do not sing with a cold that has caused hoarseness or involves the larynx, and sing as little as possible with any kind of respiratory infection. Unless there is a medical or physical problem, following these sensible rules will allow you many more years of good, healthy singing.

1. Murdock, "Born to Sing," 136.
2. Brown, *Discover Your Voice*, 70.
3. Ibid., 91.
4. Sataloff, "Professional Singers: The Science and Art of Clinical Care," 253.
5. Brown, *Discover Your Voice*, 97.
6. Ibid.
7. Sataloff, "Professional Singers: The Science and Art of Clinical Care," 256.

# 16
## The Alexander Technique
## Applied to Singing

*"When tension is pointed out to us, our effort is to go immediately
from wrong to right. Our desire is to correct ourselves in a moment
even though it has taken us years to get it wrong."*
—*F. M. Alexander*

A well-known actor in Australia and England, known mostly for his
Shakespearean roles, F. Mathias Alexander developed the Alexander
Technique around 1900. Afflicted by periodic loss of his voice, for which
medical treatments gave only temporary relief, Alexander suspected that the
problem might be the result of something he was doing with his vocal
mechanism. He began using three mirrors in which he could observe himself at different angles. He discovered that what he was doing wrong did not
stop (or start) with his vocal mechanism, but involved a pattern of malfunc-
tioning throughout his entire body. He also realized that what he felt he was
doing was quite different from what he observed in the mirror. His custom-
ary use of his body—although it caused his vocal problems—felt natural
and "right," while new and improved habits at first felt strange.

In the course of solving his problems, he developed a new approach to
physical education and health, an approach that has enabled thousands of
men, women, and children to use their bodies with ease, grace, flexibility,
and freedom from strain. Alexander established a school in London, and the
Technique has since spread throughout the world.

It took Alexander nine years of painstaking observation and study in front
of the three-way mirror. In addition to observing himself, he began watching other people, and he saw that most people had similar problems. He dis-

covered that when he pointed out tension to a person, the person wanted to go immediately from wrong to right—to correct in a moment what had taken years to get wrong. Alexander believed one must first put the mind in "neutral" and "do nothing," then work to redirect thoughts and efforts. He maintained that by learning to inhibit habitual responses, a person can make remarkable changes relatively quickly and easily. Otherwise, trying to overlay a new response on top of the old one produces conflict. In the "neutral" or "non-doing" phase, the conscious messages or new instructions sent from the mind to the body parts concerned quickly replace the habitual wrong way of using the body. Alexander called it reeducation rather than education, because reeducation implies learning something once known. Thus, the Alexander Technique really involves unlearning poor habits and poor responses, and relearning the original good use and good responses.[1]

Jonathan Drake suggests that you use the phrase "to let go" to help find the neutral phase. "Saying 'to let' gives time to delay the habitual response, perhaps for the moment, perhaps indefinitely."[2] He then offers specific phrases that one can use to undo subconscious habits and release the resulting tensions.

| Effects of Subconscious Habits | Directions to Be Given |
| --- | --- |
| Stiffened neck | To let the neck be free |
| Head retracted into shoulders | To let the head go forward and up |
| Back shortened and narrowed | To let the back lengthen and widen |

As singers seek to express the emotions of the words and music, they often stiffen the neck and shoulders and tighten the throat. In order to respond to the emotion of songs and arias, singers need to have a free voice. The Alexander Technique teaches that you can't control one set of muscles without involving the use of other muscles. This induces self-awareness and greatly benefits singers. Learning to release tension from the involved muscles is of utmost importance for singers as well as instrumentalists. People don't do what they feel to be wrong when they are trying to be right. Bad use cannot be modified; it must be stopped and replaced by something new and better. This does not mean that you abandon the traditional techniques of singing. The Alexander Technique—designed to induce the best possible relationship between the head, neck, torso, and legs at any given moment— will make for an open throat and freedom of the muscles of support.

Primary Control, a term basic to the Alexander Technique, refers to this relationship of the neck, head, and spine that enables one to achieve optimum use of the body. Alexander Technique lessons teach the student to develop and maintain Primary Control. Through lessons the student becomes conscious of poor habits of posture and carriage, learns to inhibit them, and learns to replace them with improved habits. Students find that they make progress in the areas of the neck, head, and spine simultaneously.

The Technique is not a system of exercises. That may make it seem suspiciously simple, but in fact, it requires something that is—at least at first— much more difficult than exercise: concentrated thought. The Technique requires that the student make a conscious decision to do nothing. The teacher then presents the student with a series of verbal directions which the student repeats to himself. These directions describe what should take place in the body during movement. While the student repeats these instructions, the teacher guides him through repeated new experiences both in movement and at rest. With the aid of a mirror the student sees, as did Alexander, that he or she cannot rely on present feelings as a guide to good use. The teacher helps the student discover what good use is and acts as a corrective guide until the student no longer needs one.

A person becomes so accustomed to the usual way of doing things that it "feels right," even when it is not. Any other way of doing things, even when more efficient, is bound to feel "wrong." Remember the old nursery rhyme: "There was a crooked man who had a crooked house who walked a crooked mile"? Any exercise engaged in to correct an old habit is likely to be done in the wrong way. Because it is done in the habitual (wrong) way, it will fail to correct anything.

Edward Maisel in his introduction on Alexander's collected writings, defines good use as follows:

But how then do we acquire a better use of ourselves, and with it an improved approach to the activities of living? If behavior is mainly movement, what is the prerequisite of good movement? As early as 1907, Alexander identified this prerequisite with the greatest lengthening of the spine possible in whatever we may be doing. It was this vertebral lengthening in activity which he then called "the true and primary movement in each and every act."[3]

Stransky defines this "true and primary movement" and stresses the importance of lengthening the spine:

> The true and primary movement in each and every act refers to the lengthening of the spine. This says to me that before and during every activity, every act, you need that lengthening of the spine so that the use of the body will be good. Now in the term "primary control" Alexander was referring not only to the relationship of the head and neck to the spine, but that the head is to be poised lightly on the top of the spine to allow it to lengthen. That indicates to me that you are actually controlling the way you function, whether you are at rest or in movement. Also, the term "primary control" gives a picture of the head literally leading everything. This seems logical and in order. Again, let it be understood, that when Alexanderians use the term "control" it is not meant as a muscular control which would involve rigidity or forcing. The control comes through thinking. I want to stress this, Alexander often used a phrase to describe his technique: "psycho-physical re-education with conscious control in the use of the self." The term "conscious control" is a key term, it means that you control through thinking—through conscious thoughts. You control with your brain—your brain is going to control everything by the way it gives orders to the body, the head leads the torso upwards.[4]

Singers must have a "kinesthetic awareness." It is through this sense that we are aware of any tensions or pressures in our bodies. The Alexander Technique teaches a way to adapt ourselves to our new way of doing. It simply begins with "not doing" as we inhibit our old, tense ways of "doing" the most simple acts such as standing or sitting.

Before you climb a flight of stairs, stop a second and think, "neck release, head forward and up, back to lengthen and widen." Even without lessons you should feel a sense of lightness and ease in the effort it takes to climb the stairs. When we become skilled at letting these concepts precede our actions, we have a new awareness of the relationship between our head, neck, and spine which gives a feeling of lightness and ease in the handling of our bodies. There is an overall flexibility and ease of movement, greater freedom in the action of our eyes, less tension in the jaw, more relaxation in the tongue and throat, and deeper breathing because of the effect of the new alignment on our diaphragm. There is also a sense of weightlessness that requires less effort to move our arms and legs. Activity now flows more freely with a noticeable release of tension.

I was introduced to the Alexander Technique while I was teaching at the University of Utah. Several students told me that their theory teacher told them about a better way to use their minds and bodies. At their suggestion, I introduced myself to their theory teacher, James Drake. James was working on his DMA in organ performance and pedagogy at the university. He had been studying in England where he heard about the Alexander Technique. James generously gave me several lessons and I quickly was able to define tensions in my body when I was teaching. Occasionally he would drop into my studio unannounced, lightly put his hands on my neck and head to give my body the message to "let go" with the "head forward and up" and I would immediately feel a release of tension. I had been having so much tension that it was causing stiffness and pain in my neck and back and increased nervousness when performing.

The sessions seemed so subtle. The hardest part was to not "make" the movement or to anticipate what he was doing. He asked me to think the directions and not to do them while he was lightly touching the back of my neck. At first, I didn't understand what James was doing, but at the end of the session I felt much lighter than usual. After a few sessions I was walking and climbing stairs with much less effort, sleeping better, and finding once again the ease of singing. I discovered that as I made suggestions to my students, I would try to silently help them and I would physically tense up in the process. By practicing letting my mind give the message to my body to "let go," I soon learned to let go of the tension.

Many universities have Alexander teachers, as do most schools of music and theatre. Private instructors are available in most areas. Professionals in the medical field also use the Technique. Alexander was awarded the Nobel Foundation Prize in 1973. It is a very important part of my teaching in helping students to release tensions by mental control. I did not try to incorporate them into my teaching, however, until I had many lessons from Dr. Drake and others. I strongly encourage you to find an Alexander teacher to learn these skills.

While writing this chapter, I was dealing with a great deal of pain in my left shoulder, upper back, and arm. I had tried to find relief through sessions with a chiropractor, a massage therapist, and several other alternative therapies. After writing the above instructions, I realized that I had not been applying the concepts in this chapter to myself in teaching and everyday living situations. I took a few moments to apply them to myself as I had learned to do while working with an Alexander teacher. Within a few minutes the pain and tension were gone. I have since done the routine each day and am amazed at how the pain has lessened. Knowledge is of no use if it isn't applied.

**Exercises:**
The following instructions are typical of the first lessons with an Alexander teacher. It is best to lie on the floor with a book about 1 or 2 inches thick under your head. Keep your knees bent and feel as if the small of your back is "melting" into the floor. After you have become skillful with this while lying on the floor, this exercise can also be done while sitting in a chair. Say to yourself:

• Neck release…to let the head come forward and up out of the shoulders …to let the back lengthen and widen.

• Neck release…to let the head come forward and up…to let the back lengthen and widen…to let the shoulders lengthen and widen and fan out against the floor.

• Neck release…to let the head come forward and up out of shoulders…to let the back lengthen and widen…to let the right arm lengthen out of free shoulder…to let the lower right arm lengthen out of free elbow…to let the fingers lengthen out of free hand into infinity…(repeat with left arm).

- Hips to lengthen out of free waist.

- Right thigh to lengthen out of free hip.

- Lower right leg to lengthen out of free knee.

- Right foot to lengthen into infinity.

- Left thigh to lengthen out of free hip.

- Lower left leg to lengthen out of free knee.

- Left foot to lengthen into infinity.

- Let the knees fall up to the ceiling. Keeping the lengthening of the back, lift the weight off of the hips, and rotate the hips forward to flatten the back against the floor.

- Repeat these instructions from the beginning. This time when you focus on the legs, put them down slowly, one at a time and push the heel of each foot toward the wall.

- Roll over to your side and help yourself to a standing position by pushing yourself up with your hands and arms. Don't try to sit up immediately from the lying-on-the-floor position.

1. David, "An Interview with Judith Stransky," 7.
2. Drake, *Body Know How*, 1991.
3. Maisel, *The Resurrection of the Body*, xxii.
4. David, "An Interview with Judith Stransky," 7.

# 17
# Choral Application

*"Since singing is so good a thing*
*I wish all men would learn to sing."*
*–William Byrd*

For many people who love to sing, the choral rehearsal provides their singular source of vocal training. Choral directors, therefore, bear the responsibility for the vocal development and vocal health of the individual singers in the choir. A conscientious choral director will actively teach correct principles of singing, helping singers to develop correct habits and free unwanted tension.

The ideal time for vocal development and training is the beginning of rehearsal when singers are fresh and alert. Starting rehearsal with carefully selected vocalises helps singers to become more kinesthetically aware of correct singing habits. In addition, warm-ups help free the voice and energize the body and breath. Conductors can adapt most of the vocalises in this book to help their choirs achieve this purpose. As choral singers learn to sing with a healthy technique and without tension, they will achieve a more beautiful choral tone, increased vocal range, greater agility in melismatic passages, better blending of vowels, and increased vocal health and endurance.

## Considering the Child and Adolescent Voice in Choral Singing
Sung out at 17? This is often the case with high school singers who might have had a professional career or a lifetime of enjoyable singing, had they received better guidance in their formative years. High school choral directors can be sensitive to the young voice, ensuring the student a lifetime of healthy singing.

Vocal problems begin well before age 17. Singing at the elementary level is suffering as well. I remember one very prominent music educator saying a decade or so ago, "For some reason, and we don't know why, young people's voices are getting lower, so we will have to lower the keys of the music that they sing." The reason *is* known. Children listen to and imitate the rock stars, who all sing in the belt voice. They seldom hear good examples illustrating correct use of the head voice or light mechanism and are encouraged to sing louder, which they do by yelling the song. Children's music is often written low so they only sing with the throat adjusted to a yelling position. For all of these reasons, children never learn to make the adjustment from the heavy mechanism to the light mechanism.

Singing is a primal form of communication and expression for children. Most communities have children's choirs that can foster good singing and musical skills. Before choosing a choir for their children, parents should attend performances and talk to qualified vocal teachers.

Repertoire and style are also important things to consider. Some choirs teach children to sing in their light voices and choose mostly classics, art songs, and folk ballads for repertoire. (Singing in the light voice is not the same as overly soft singing which is devitalized, breathy, and unhealthy.) Other choirs use the belt or yelling style, which can amount to vocal abuse. I cannot stress enough the need to choose a choir that teaches children to use their voices safely and healthily. If children are taught to use their voices correctly, a good choir can be a great experience for them.

As I audition and adjudicate young people each year at various musical festivals and competitions, I hear more and more evidence of vocal fatigue and strain. I recall one of my young students always coming to her lessons sounding vocally tired and a little hoarse. When I inquired about her singing habits, she said, "I think I am just tired." Then she explained, "I sing in two choir classes each day—A Cappella and Madrigals. In Madrigals we are doing a lot of pop music and my throat hurts when I sing that style. Besides that, I was in the chorus of a professional musical production that ran nearly every night for two weeks. Before that, there were three weeks of rehearsal every night so I never got to bed before 12:30 or 1:00 a.m. Now, I am in the school musical that rehearses after school and Saturdays. I don't know what I will do when we start our Christmas performances. Our teacher said that some days we have as many as five performances."

This is simply too much singing—too much use of the voice even for mature artists who know how to use their voices correctly. Professional singers seldom use their voices more than an hour and a half at a time. Even at that, they are not singing continually. Such is the case with oratorios and operas; soloists rest their voices during the choral numbers and other soloists' arias. Far from mature, my young student has been averaging at least five hours of singing a day. This kind of schedule in her teens could cause permanent damage. She has a very beautiful voice that could bring years of pleasure to her and to others. What a tragedy if she sacrifices a lifetime of singing enjoyment for a few years of high school fun.

This is not an isolated case. It is repeated every year in private vocal studios. The sad sequel to the story is a twenty-two-year-old singer with the remnants of a once beautiful voice that cries, "I don't know what happened! I was one of the soloists in high school (where she belted out the lead in *How to Succeed in Business Without Even Trying*) and I just can't sing at all anymore. Can you help me?" Sometimes yes, and sometimes no.

In too many cases, the vocal habits and wrong use of the musculature are so established that I cannot help. Most of the time, with a skilled teacher and the proper vocal exercises to retrain the singing mechanism, the problem is reversible if the student is determined to succeed and practices diligently. It takes years of therapeutic work that could have been spent in enjoyable singing.

What about the pop/rock singers who sing professionally and never seem to tire? You will find that they usually have a limited range and are not able to sing with any dynamic variation. They can sing only one style and their careers are often short-lived. I once heard someone ask a prominent laryngologist about this type of singing at a vocal workshop. He responded that if you think the pop singers have survived, you should see all the damaged voices that he sees.

Most high school choral directors are very dedicated, talented teachers who want the best for their students. Over the many years I have been teaching, I have highly encouraged my students to be in their school choirs because of the many things they learn from their dedicated choral directors. They learn fine repertoire, interpretation of musical styles, musicianship, punctuality, discipline, and how to respect others' talents and time.

What can choral directors, who are dedicated to young singers' health, do to reverse this damaging trend? First, consider not allowing young singers to be in more than one performing organization. In some schools, choirs and singing groups are status symbols and this influences the students nearly as much as their love of singing.

Second, with all of the fine choral music available, do not choose music that is too loud or stays too high for too long. A fine young tenor, who is also a high school choral director, was singing in the chorus of Beethoven's Ninth Symphony with a professional symphony. He got so carried away with the music that he was over-singing. He felt something pop in his throat and could no longer sing. He called me the next day and I advised him to go to a laryngologist who found that he had a hemorrhage on his vocal folds. He continued teaching school and singing in a professional choir without giving his voice time to heal. A year later he totally lost his voice. When he called me the second time he could barely talk. He went again to the doctor who scoped his cords and found a large polyp, which had to be surgically removed. After complete voice rest and speech therapy he has recovered and is teaching and singing again. I hope he now has more respect for the health of his voice.

In my opinion, high school or university choirs should never sing Beethoven's Ninth Symphony and other taxing oratorios and masses. They are too intense, too long, too high, and too loud for young voices. So much suitable and wonderful music is available: Mozart's *Coronation Mass* and *Requiem*, Haydn's *Creation*, Schubert's *Mass in C*, Mozart's *Mass in C Minor*, Vaughan-Williams' *Hodie* and John Rutter's *Requiem,* to name a few.

Third, be sure each young singer is singing the right voice part. Always test voices carefully, choosing vocalises that work from the highest pitch level down as well as from the lowest pitch level up. Have students sing the vowel [u] in a light head voice on a descending scale, then alternate to [ɑ] and [o]. This helps you to hear where the natural transition occurs, preventing them from pulling the heavy mechanism past the first *passaggio* causing their voice to "break" or "crack." The second *passaggio* will give a good indication of whether the singer should be singing soprano, alto, tenor or bass. (See Chapters 9 and 10.)

Some singers will need to change sections during the year as their voices mature and change. Watch for any visible signs of strain. When singing out of their comfortable range, students will look uncomfortable and tend to tip their heads back, jut their jaws forward, and tighten their throats. Never allow a young woman to sing tenor—even if her voice goes easily down to D3 or E3. The sound is not right for your choir's needs. It can also limit female singers to the point that they will never be able to shift out of the heavy mechanism, thus severely limiting the possibility of being a solo performer.

Fourth, encourage your students not to sing if they have colds or laryngitis. If they need to learn new music, they can do so by concentrated observing. If such an illness happens to come at a busy performance time such as Christmas or spring festivals, excuse them from the performances. Have them sit away from the choir in rehearsals to stop the spread of their germs. Singing with a sore or infected throat is like skiing on a broken leg. An athlete is excused from playing or competing until the healing is complete. Shouldn't a singer whose instrument is so delicate and needs such fine-tuning have the same consideration? We should stress to our students the need to take special care of their health. So many times I have seen high school choirs traveling to performances without coats at various venues in the middle of the winter, often walking several blocks in a snowstorm at freezing temperatures. Is it not "cool" to wear coats these days?

Fifth, if your school performs musicals, choose those appropriate to their development with lovely, lyric songs such as *Brigadoon, Music Man, Carousel,* or *Fiddler On The Roof.* Even if a voice sounds mature at 17 or 18, a singer is still in the cradle stage of vocal maturity. Nothing ruins the immature female voice faster than trying to emulate the Streisand sound, without having the

Streisand throat and maturity. After a young voice belts a few roles, the adjustment into the lyric style is difficult and vice versa. Avoid shows such as *Mame, Hello, Dolly!* and other musicals written in the belt style. Annie in *Annie, Get Your Gun* sings every style from belting to ballad. The part was written for Ethel Merman when she was in her late thirties or forties. By then she had developed a wobble in her voice, but she was such a popular performer who audiences loved for her personality that she could get away with bad singing.

Finally, limit the time of singing in rehearsal by doing some fun physical activity such as mirroring. Have choir members choose a partner and stand face to face. Then have them put their arms out, hands not quite touching. Choose one to lead and the other to follow exactly what the leader does. After a few minutes have them change leaders. Next, choose one to be a puppet and the other to move the arms, body, legs, hands, etc. with no resistance on the part of the one playing the puppet. Change positions. Next, have them close their eyes and have each one hum a little tune. Instruct them to walk around while humming and see if they can find their partner by the tune they are humming. These activities teach how to trust each other and work as a team.

As music educators, we must carefully analyze our role. Are we here to serve the needs of the students, or are they here to serve us in our eagerness to create the right image for our school and for ourselves as teachers? Could we back up a little and counsel the eager students who want to be in everything to slow down a bit, so as not to harm their chances for future singing, even if we need their voices and personalities in all of our groups?

How many potential singers do we bypass by giving the more assertive students all of the opportunities? Ideally, the experience of discovering the wonderful world of music should be made available to all students. It is a life-changing experience that can enrich their entire lives.

## Choral Considerations for Any Age
Private voice teachers and choral directors need to see eye-to-eye with regard to vocal techniques that allow and encourage healthy vocal production. That said, the choral director faces many challenges in training voices during a

choral rehearsal that are not present in the private studio. Choral directors are limited because of the sheer number of voices that they must deal with simultaneously. Singers in a choir often come from a wide array of musical backgrounds and may have very diverse vocal needs. One may sing with a weak, breathy tone, while another sings with a pushed tone. Furthermore, choral directors might fail to notice a significant problem in an individual voice because it is hidden by the other voices.

Since the choral tone is no better than the sum of its parts, choral directors must attend to the development of the individual voices within the choir. One way to help facilitate this is by reducing the number of voices you are working with at a time. This is most easily accomplished by holding regular sectional rehearsals. In sectionals, singers generally feel more motivated because they can more easily hear improvements in their own voices with fewer people singing. It also is much easier for a director to see and hear what is happening in individual voices and to give personal feedback.

Having a vocal coach associated with the choir is one possible rehearsal model that facilitates this kind of sectional work. While the conductor rehearses the choir, the vocal coach can regularly, and on a rotating basis, take out a subset of the choir to work on vocal technique, applying the technique directly to the literature being prepared. Alternately, if the director feels he wants to maintain more personal influence over the vocal development of the singers, he can conduct the sectionals himself while allowing an assistant conductor to rehearse the main body of the choir.

Even when rehearsing the entire choir, a conductor can reduce the number of individuals she is working with by asking one section (or individual) to sing a particular vocalise or musical passage. It then becomes easier to give meaningful feedback and creates a great deal of motivation to improve since the choir members have an audience. The rest of the choir is learning, too, by watching.

At all times during a choral rehearsal, the director should be watching and listening for clues about vocal production. Do the individual singers display posture that looks balanced and free? Can you see or hear improper and unnecessary tension in the tongue or throat? Once a director recognizes a particular vocal weakness in one or more singers in the choir, he can use that information in selecting vocalises to use at the beginning of the next rehearsal.

## Beginning the Rehearsal: A Suggested Routine

Every choir has unique vocal needs based on the ages and training level of the individual singers. The following is a possible sequence of exercises to begin a rehearsal.

1. Posture: Choose an exercise from Chapter 2. A brief posture exercise is a great way to begin a rehearsal because it is energizing, it focuses the choir's attention, and prepares the body to sing.

2. Breath Preparation/Management and Vocal Onset: Choose one or two vocalises from Chapters 3 and 4. Any vocalise using a lip buzz is great for choirs because it energizes and connects the breath to the voice (see Exercise 4g). If a vocalise is too challenging or complex, adapt it as necessary for the needs of the choir.

3. Resonance: Choose a vocalise from Chapter 6. Use it to develop a better *chiaroscuro* (warm/bright, balanced, and resonant) tone with your choir.

4. Diction: Choose a vocalise from Chapter 7. Use it for unifying the five primary vowels and teaching efficiency in production of text. Exercise 7b is an excellent exercise for working with vowels.

5. Range: Choose a vocalise from Chapter 10.

6. Application: Choose a short passage from your repertoire (possibly one that presented a vocal challenge at the last rehearsal) and see if the choir can apply healthy vocal technique to the passage. Give feedback and try it several times if necessary. Consider trying the passage in different keys.

Choral singers may be resistant to vocal exercises, especially if they have never experienced them. Clearly communicating the purpose of each vocalise can ease feelings of frustration and self-consciousness. Vocalises do much more than "warm-up" the voice; they train correct habits of singing. Taking time to sing vocalises also communicates to the choir the conductor's commitment to healthy vocal technique and beautiful tone.

Sometimes choral conductors, in their rush to achieve a good sound, create stumbling blocks when they emphasize tone before technique. If a choral conductor has neglected to train healthy singing technique, the tone will inevitably suffer. Some conductors then attempt to "patch up" poor tone quality with a "quick fix" like "use more support!" or "raise your eyebrows!"

Conductors often insist on a particular tone quality (brighter, darker, straight tone, etc.), without providing the technical foundation for achieving such tone. Unfortunately, insisting on a certain tone or using a "quick fix" is likely to encourage improper and unnecessary tension, and will cover up fundamental problems of technique. For example, if a conductor insists on a brighter tone, singers may attempt to achieve this through tongue tension. Furthermore, in a choral setting the "quick fix" approach is especially dangerous because a conductor cannot monitor each singer to make sure that instructions have been applied in a healthy way.

A better approach is to place first priority on building a healthy singing technique while trusting that excellent tone will be the result. If the tone is not satisfactory, use this as a clue that technique needs more work. Try to get to the root of the problem: Is there tension in the tongue? Is the breath energy sufficient? Is the jaw released?

Choral directors can very successfully apply many of the teaching tools found throughout this book because they allow the singers to monitor themselves and to become their own teachers. For example, a conductor can ask the choir to place a thumb underneath the chin to monitor for tongue tension, or a conductor might ask the choir to gently press in with two fingers at the corners of the mouth (leaving the tongue forward and free) to help release the jaw. Building a kinesthetic awareness of healthy singing technique in the individual singer will go a long way towards achieving a beautiful choral tone.

The emphasis of some directors to sing with a "straight tone" takes the vibrancy and ring out of choir members' singing. When used as a standard for desired tone, the singer often tightens his throat and raises the larynx to produce straight tone. Small instances of straight tone or whisper tone for emotional communication is very different than asking singers to consistently remove the vibrancy and efficiency of the naturally vibrating voice. A good choral sound certainly cannot have voices with many different vibrato rates that seem to go from the "bleat" to the "wobble." Choral directors, however, need to find a better term such as a "more pure tone," or a tone that is vibrant, but without an oscillating vibrato.

Correctly trained singers who are willing to listen and adapt to the sounds around them will naturally blend with other voices of a choir. The major problems occur when the trained singer has an inflexible technique that cannot adapt to the many styles and periods of choral music. The free and vibrant tone, not overly dark or bright, of a well-trained singer will blend and enhance the quality of the choir.

# 18
## Making the Most of
## Voice Lessons

*"Let us make a comparison: is a person who is strongly drawn to the piano
necessarily a virtuoso? No, to the desire must be added serious study,
in order to completely develop into artistry. Therefore, how can one
expect that the voice (which is the most beautiful, but at the same time
the finest and most delicate instrument) will reveal all the passions
of the soul without thorough study of its technique?"*
—G.B. Lamperti

## To the Student

*Choosing a teacher*

Choosing the vocal teacher who is right for your needs should be made very
carefully. No one is the right teacher for everyone who wants to study
singing. When you hear a singer who sings well, it is a good idea to ask them
with whom they study. Try to attend a recital of that teacher's students. If
you feel that everyone is singing freely and with a technique that allows them
to sing easily and expressively, ask if the teacher will let you observe some
lessons. If most of the singers are singing with a beautiful, resonant ringing
tone it is evident that they are being taught properly and are establishing a
technique for the foundation that will serve them for a lifetime of beautiful
singing.

When you have found a teacher and started lessons, you need to do your
part by diligently practicing the vocalises. After a reasonable amount of time,
you should evaluate how things are going. If your voice tires easily, if it
doesn't feel free and comfortable when you sing, and you have not noticed
an improvement in quality, it might be wise to find a new teacher.

*Trusting your teacher, singing the right repertoire*

Once you feel confident you are in the right studio it is time to trust your teacher. Trust her ability to give instructions on how to correct and improve your technique. The tools in this book only work as students allow themselves to experience different sensations and release of tensions. This requires being open-minded to new ideas, including a willingness to accept new concepts and sensations. A student must recognize that when they feel a different sensation, usually more freedom and less local control, the new feeling usually means something is changing for good.

I had a new student come to me completely discouraged with her current voice and technique. As I listened to her, she was singing everything like a Valkyrie. She was driving the voice and muscularly manufacturing every tone. We worked to free the instrument by letting her voice spin on the breath instead of pushing with the breath. She commented that her voice felt very different, but she didn't accept the change saying, "It doesn't feel like my voice." To my ears her voice became more warm and ringing instead of strident and wobbly. To her, these new sensations were different and therefore wrong. It takes patience and practice to move from the old to the new.

Students must also adhere to the teacher's recommendation for repertoire. I remember when I fell in love with Mimì. I was about 14. I heard *La Bohème* on a Metropolitan Opera broadcast and I thought to myself that I didn't think I could live if I didn't sing that role. Well, I'm still alive and I never was able to perform Mimì. My voice was properly classified as a lyric-coloratura; Mimì is a big, warm lyric soprano. Later on, my mother bought the score of *La Bohème* and I would sit at the piano for hours playing the wonderful music and singing along as if it was written for me. I didn't even realize that singing such dramatic music was not right for my voice. I just wanted to sing music that touched my soul. I used to think that I was born a violin and I wanted to be a cello. I nearly ruined the violin trying to be a cello. Singing such music as well as singing with a little jazz band in high school (where I constantly pulled the heavy mechanism too high) caused serious *passaggio* problems and weakness in my middle voice. While trying to restore my own voice, I became fascinated with how the voice worked and this started my interest in teaching.

Over my many years of teaching I have had students bring music that is not suitable for their particular voice. Perhaps they have been given the lead role in a school musical, have been assigned music by a conductor, or have chosen music that they "just have to sing." Sometimes they have been resistant to my advice to avoid certain literature or roles. If they persist in singing music that is too heavy or beyond their technical ability, their voice can get out of balance and wrong muscular habits will develop.

Lamperti makes this statement about singing the wrong repertoire,

> In Germany it is not only the true sopranos who have almost disappeared but also the tenors, because a German tenor who cannot sing Wagner cannot obtain an engagement or position of importance. Therefore the singers strain their voices: they force themselves in order to sing the Wagner repertory. It would be much better, if tenors who did not possess the vocal resources for Wagnerian opera would refrain completely from singing that repertory. The Wagnerian operas demand powerful tenors who can sing the recitative with pompous voice; nevertheless, tenors who possess only pretty, fresh, agreeable but weak voices, insist on singing Wagner…A tenor possesses the most delicate type of voice: it demands a very earnest and carefully prepared course of study. But most tenors in Germany sing with the emission of a baritone because they then believe themselves to be Wagnerian tenors. They force the middle voice and do not realize that the mal-treated voice will, with time, become old and tired.[1]

The same is true of the lyric soprano voice. Lamperti continues:

> Why are the voices of Patti and Madame Sembrich so well preserved? Because they sing only the repertory which suits their voices. In 1885 I was in Paris in order to assist Sembrich at her debut in "Traviata" and "Lucia." One day she told me that she would like to sing "Faust." I protested energetically and urgently advised her to sing only the operas of her repertory. (She would have ruined her voice in "Faust" and in a short time would have become a singer like thousands of others.)[2]

Singing the lead in musical theatre or opera is so much fun it is difficult for a student not to accept a particular role that they have been given. However, many singers have ruined their voices in the process because it meant so much to them to be the lead in the high school musical or the university opera production. Sacrificing your voice simply isn't worth it.

To maintain the health and longevity of your voice, it is necessary to only sing roles that are safe for you, roles that are in the right tessitura and style. Opera roles must be sung in the original key while art songs can be sung in various keys. However, just because a singer *can* sing a song doesn't mean that they *should* sing it. Much depends on the color and weight of the voice. For example, art songs such as Schubert's "Gretchen am Spinnrade" and "Erlkönig," and Brahms' "Die Mainacht" and "Von Ewiger Liebe" must be sung by darker, heavier voices. These art songs and many others simply don't work in a light, lyric voice. Trust your teacher and work with her closely in choosing the repertoire that is suitable for your voice.

### Taking notes at lessons

It is discouraging for a teacher when a student achieves a breakthrough at a lesson, only to come the following week having lost or even forgotten much or all of the progress made. Make it easy for yourself to retain what you learn by taking notes during your lesson. This valuable lesson time is a window of opportunity for building a secure technique so make the most of it. Don't rely on your memory to recall what you learn. Often writing just a word or two describing the sensation or the thought is all that is needed to remind you of what you learned. In addition, the process of writing helps put the thoughts experienced at each lesson into a different, deeper sense.

I also encourage students to record their lessons. Listening to a recording of your lesson reminds you of what took place. Be careful not to react to what you hear and try to muscularly fix the problem. Listen instead to your teacher's instructions and try to repeat the sensations you had at your lesson rather than physically correcting what you hear. Recording lessons also can help you to monitor and evaluate your progress. Depending on where you practice, it is often more expedient to just glance at your notes than to try to find what you want to hear on the recording.

### Practice

Do not wait too long to practice after a lesson. If you wait a day or two, you will likely forget much of what you experienced. If your lesson is during the day, take some time during the evening of that same day to review some of the vocal issues you focused on in your lesson. In general, I think two or three shorter practice sessions spaced throughout the day are better than one long session. The more often you can revisit the vocal exercises and tools being used to train your voice, the faster you will develop the correct habits of singing and the sooner the new habits will become your own. The great violin teacher Dr. Shinichi Suzuki said, "Ability equals knowledge plus 10,000 times." If you must do your practicing all in one block of time, alternate your practicing between singing and mental preparation, such as memorization, working on interpretation by studying the text, or simply singing through the song or aria in your mind.

Many great athletes and musicians alike rely on mental practicing as a powerful tool to enhance their performance. Remember, when the mind has a clear objective or target outcome, the body will follow, often exceeding our own expectations of what we thought we could do. If you want to work on singing with a better legato line, for example, close your eyes and try to hear in your mind exactly the kind of tone that you want. Take your time and make the sound as real as possible. The clearer the mental sound, the better your final results will be. Once you have the sound securely created in your mind, then decide that this is the sound you want to make. Now get out of the way and let the body sing. If it isn't perfect the first time, perhaps you need to imagine the sound again, or perhaps the body just needs a few more tries. Mental practicing is particularly valuable because it can accelerate your progress. It is also healthy for the voice because it provides an opportunity for the voice to rest. A famous singer once said, "Think for twenty minutes, sing for ten."

No singer will make significant progress without dedication to consistent practicing. It is important to practice intelligently. Find a place where you feel emotionally safe to sing with a full tone and to experiment with your voice. Some sounds we make while practicing are not what a listener would call "beautiful singing." If you hold back in case someone is listening you will suppress the energy you need to really connect your voice to the breath. In addition to practicing the calisthenics of the vocalises, also tune in to the vibrations and sensations in your body. Always sing with your heart and soul, even on the vocalises. Instruments don't have words to portray their music like singers do. Let every sound that comes from your singing have meaning and feeling.

*Your voice is unique*

Too often singers try so hard to sound like someone else. On more than one occasion a student has said to me, "Can you help me to sound like Renée Fleming?" or some other famous singer. It certainly can be beneficial to listen to and learn from other excellent singers, but be careful not to imitate the sound. Hearing a fine singer can give the mind a template for what beautiful singing sounds like and can give you ideas for shaping a phrase, language inflection, and for qualities you want to develop in your own voice. For example, you might think, "I'd like to have a deeper, brighter sound in my low range like Bryn Terfel." It is good to listen and be inspired, but avoid trying to duplicate or reproduce another singer's unique sound. Besides being potentially harmful to the voice, it simply is not possible. Since no two bodies are identical, no two voices will be identical either. When singers try to make their voice sound like someone else, tension and accompanying vocal problems are bound to occur.

Remember that your subconscious mind instinctively knows how to produce a free, beautiful sound. An instinctive singer just lets the voice sing. As you practice getting in touch with your "singing instincts," you will discover your own unique and beautiful sound.

I once taught a young soprano who had the opportunity to go to Europe to study during her sophomore year of college. At the time she was singing with a free-flowing, ringing tone. I considered her to be an instinctive singer who just needed guidance and direction. She was beginning to develop a warm, full sound, although she had a tendency to want to make her voice bigger. Unfortunately, the director of the opera program at the university she attended had told her that she would never make it as an opera singer because her voice was not "big" enough. She studied overseas for several years where her teachers emphasized making her voice bigger. Part of her motivation was to prove this director wrong so she focused on the size of the voice rather than the beauty.

When she returned from Europe, she came to sing for me. I was distressed at the change in her voice. She was literally forcing herself to sing by pushing with the breath and tensing the abdominal and buttock muscles to the point that they were shaking. The voice sounded forced and strident, and what she considered passion and emotion in her singing caused a pained expression on her lovely face. Seeing her working so hard made listeners uncomfortable. An audience does not want to be involved with the process of the physical effort it takes to sing. They want to be moved by the beauty of the words and music and to be thrilled by the sound and deep emotional soul of the singer. Her voice had lost its free flowing beauty. She had lost some of her high notes, and the ring and spin were gone. At one lesson when she was having a problem letting her voice go, I said to her, "Use your natural instinct to sing." She replied, "I don't have an instinct any more." What a sad commentary. She had tried so hard to make her voice big and impressive and to emotionally and physically give her all that she had lost the wonderful, natural voice with which she was blessed.

## To the Teacher

*The positive approach*

The studio needs to be a warm, safe, and nurturing environment. If we always encourage, acknowledge improvement, and consistently provide the best instruction and tools for developing a good technique, our students will progress. If our attitude is negative and our response is critical, just as a flower cannot flourish without good soil, water, and sun, the young singer will not bloom into his full potential. Some young singers are so sensitive to the positive or negative energy of the teacher, we must watch our facial expressions and our gestures as well as the words we use to make a point.

It is useless to point out a problem if we do not have a solution. Instead of pointing out what is wrong, try first to give a positive suggestion of what you would like to happen to improve the tone. Use one of the tools in this book and see if the problem can fix itself.

Students need to feel positive and optimistic after a voice lesson. Teachers can encourage this by being supportive and focusing on how the voice is improving. At the same time, students need to know they can trust their teacher's positive feedback because it is always sincere. We should never say something sounds good when it does not. However, we can look for what is going well, and take time to point that out. We should listen for the most beautiful part of the voice and encourage the rest of the voice to emulate that sound. When students feel positive about their singing, they are more likely to sing without tension. A singer who has negative feelings about his voice will inevitably tighten muscles for fear that things will go wrong.

*Abuse*

I recently had a call from a former student who was awarded a substantial scholarship to a prominent school of music on the East Coast. She was discouraged and confused. Her teacher of four years had said to her just a week before her senior recital that she didn't know why, but she (the student) sang better the previous years than she did currently. She is a very talented, dedicated, hard working young lady who is trying diligently to learn and improve. She sent a CD of her recital to me and asked for my opinion of her singing. During her four years at this school she had been taught to "put the voice forward" or the *"dans la masque"* technique which had caused a high larynx as well as tongue and mylohyoid tension resulting in an over-bright tone with a bleat-like-vibrato. After four years of sincere, dedicated study, she had vocally digressed from when she started as a freshman. The teacher's comment, while true, offered just before her recital and with no suggestions for fixing the problem was discouraging and abusive.

Abuse in the vocal studio is a sad reality. *Classical Singer* magazine dedicated the entire September 2002 issue to the subject. It is disturbing to read about some singers' experiences. The articles and responses tell of verbal, physical, and sexual abuse. Why do they keep going back for lessons? Some young people come from dysfunctional homes where they have endured an abusive parent. Some have low self-esteem, which makes them more vulnerable. Some get emotionally involved with their teacher. Some are simply naïve and think that is the way it is in the "real world" of singing. It is difficult to understand, but we need to be aware that the problem is very real. It is discouraging that many of the abusers hold prominent positions in highly ranked schools and conservatories.

Because of the one-on-one contact over a long period of time, many voice teachers naturally develop a close relationship with the student. For many young people, the teacher can become a very significant part of their lives. We must be nurturing and supportive, but we need to be careful not to let students become too dependent on us. The teacher must also be careful not to develop too close a friendship with her students. I have seen many situations when it was time for students to move on to a new teacher, but they were concerned that if they changed studios it would break their present teacher's heart. Voice teachers must treat these relationships with great care.

*Focus and patience*

Building a solid singing technique occurs over months and years. There is no successful "quick fix" or shortcut to healthy, beautiful singing. A teacher should be interested instead in long-term growth, and developing a technique that will sustain a singer throughout his career. A teacher should never push a voice to develop faster than it is ready. Teachers must simply and systematically address one issue at a time, gradually building principle upon principle.

Teachers should be careful not to overload students with too many things to think about at once. When the mind becomes cluttered with too many instructions, tension can often result. Often this means a teacher must temporarily overlook certain obvious problems in order to give the student time to master a more basic issue. When working on releasing tension in the throat, it is better not to point out problems such as intonation, but get to the source. To solve the problem of singing sharp (most often caused by tension and constriction in the throat) or flat (most often caused by lack of breath energy), give suggestions and vocalises to correct the problem. Secondary problems, such as intonation, correct themselves when the source of the problem is corrected.

It usually takes a minimum of several months of lessons coupled with consistent daily practicing to replace incorrect habits. This can require a great deal of patience for a teacher. If a teacher is too anxious for a student to sound good immediately, the temptation will be very strong to take shortcuts and bypass the slow, consistent (sometimes monotonous) work of retraining the muscles. Teachers and students alike are prone to fall into the trap of wanting to correct a bad habit in a moment, but it is not possible to go immediately from wrong to right. When facing the task of retraining the body, we must first put ourselves in neutral gear. There is a period of time when the old way isn't working and the new way has not yet been accomplished.

One student in his twenties came to me with an unpleasant vocal wobble (slow vibrato) due largely to tension in the throat, jaw, and epigastrium region. He had worked with other teachers, but without success. We began working with many of the exercises in this book to release tension. As this student patiently, attentively, and consistently practiced the exercises, week by week his muscles and body began to get the new message. Gradually, he learned a new way of singing that involved less tension and that produced a freer, more beautiful tone. There were still, however, frequent relapses into the "old way." Old habits die hard, so I had to constantly listen and watch so that the moment the old habits resurfaced, I could point this out and bring him back to the "new way." After much persistence, this student is now singing largely without the tension, and the voice is beginning to sound warm and resonant.

*Help students become their own teachers*
Good teaching empowers students to become their own teachers, so that during the week they can continue to learn and make progress during their practice sessions. This can be done in a number of ways. First, try to engage a student's kinesthetic awareness. When a student makes a positive vocal change stop and ask, "What did that feel like?" or "Did that feel different?" Then let the student verbalize the experience, making the experience more concrete for the student and therefore more likely to recur at home or in the practice room. Asking a singer how something felt is better than asking "How did you do that?" because a student who remembers how good singing *feels* is more likely to recreate it than a student who tries to *make* the good singing happen again. When students, pleased at how good their voice sounded during a lesson, go home and try to make their voice sound that way again, they will often try too hard to repeat the same sensation and sound they felt and heard at their lesson. Working too hard will cause tension. The acoustical difference in the rooms where they practice will also make a difference. The student who patiently remembers the feeling and the tools that help it happen and then just "lets it happen" is more likely to progress.

A teacher can help develop students' kinesthetic awareness by having them touch various areas of the vocal mechanism (such as the thyroid cartilage or the mylohyoid muscle) to feel and monitor what is going on. I have seen many students surprised to discover how much tension they had in a certain place by simply touching the area in question while singing. Actually feeling and recognizing the tension is usually the first step in being able to let it go. Once a singer knows how to find and feel that tension, he will be able to easily monitor it himself after the lesson.

Many teachers find it useful to employ a wide array of mental imagery to teach concepts to their students. Teachers should be careful not to impose too many of their own mental images on a student. Although helpful to some students, a teacher's imagery can sometimes be misinterpreted by the student, causing him to engage the wrong muscles in an attempt to apply the image. Furthermore, an image that works for one singer may not make any sense to the mind of another. Singers should be encouraged to develop their own mental images—with the guidance of a teacher—according to their own physical sensations experienced during healthy singing. When a singer does something right, ask him what it felt like, and as he puts the sensations into words, he will be creating his own mental imagery of good singing. Listen carefully to the student's wording, and then use his own words to help remind and recreate the good results again and again. This ensures that the mental images actually work for the individual singer, thereby increasing the chances that healthy singing will continue outside of the studio and in the practice room.

*Giving career advice*
As teachers, we have a terrific responsibility to teach a secure technique of singing and to instill in each student a sense of confidence and ability. At the same time, we must guard against giving false hope that a student has the potential talent for a successful singing career. Even with talent, the percentage of those who succeed in a performance career is very low. Luck and being in the right place at the right time are huge factors in the equation. That does not mean that anyone who would like to develop their singing talent should be deprived of the opportunity to do so. Fortunately, the future of singers is not up to the teacher, but to a higher source. Our responsibility

is to give the best possible training to prepare them for whatever the future offers them as singers.

*Every voice is unique*

I believe that all teachers of singing want to give the best possible instruction to their students. However, most of us have developed our own way of getting the sound we want to hear. If our main emphasis is to make the student develop a bigger voice rather than freeing the voice, the student can put too much pressure on the vocal folds and develop tensions that can cause an uneven vibrato and stridency in the tone. We are born with the size of voice we have. A small voice can carry as well as a big voice if the resonance factor is right. It is resonance that amplifies the tone. When you sing with freedom and the right balance of the vocal mechanism and breath energy, your throat should never hurt. It might feel tired after a long choral rehearsal or practice session, as any muscle will after extended use, but if it hurts, that is a sign that something is not right.

Ideally, every voice has its own thumbprint, or its own individual color and sound. Richard DeYoung states:

> Our universe is individualized. No two leaves on a tree are alike. Of the millions of people on earth not two have the same fingerprints. Why then expect anything as individual as singing to follow a fixed pattern? With instrumentalists it is different. They may play the same piano or the same violin. But the singer is himself his instrument. His physical equipment is his healthy body, and his voice is a mental concept, an image, a sense of vocal sound.[3]

A conductor of a large professional choir who has auditioned hundreds of voices, made a comment to me that he could tell with which teacher each singer he auditioned studied. "I don't like my students to sound like each other," I told him. He replied, "We can tell your students because they all sing so freely."

I considered that a great compliment. When each voice starts sounding like every other voice that comes from the same studio, something is wrong.

Each of us has his or her own preference of what we consider a good singing tone. Perhaps we are trying to please our own taste and preference by asking for more volume, or brightness or whatever we want to hear, instead of finding the most natural, free flowing sound and ring in each individual voice.

1. Brown, *Vocal Wisdom: Maxims of Giovanni Battista Lamperti*, 2-3.
2. Ibid., 3.
3. DeYoung, *The Singer's Art*, xviii.

# Epilogue

This book is a compilation of my various learning experiences, both as a singer and teacher. I started studying when I was about 16 years old. My first two teachers taught more by imitation, often demonstrating a phrase for me and then asking me to "sing it that way." This was all very confusing, and I was soon sounding very much like the teacher. I remember a picture that one of my teachers had of a young woman with her head tipped back and her arms outstretched and a caption that said, "I will lift up my head and sing." This posture caused tension in my throat and made it difficult to sing. Another teacher put a belt around my rib cage and had me hold my ribs out so as not to drop the belt. This caused tremendous tension in my torso. Another often said, "Don't drop your dime." She meant that if you couldn't hold a dime between the muscles of the buttocks, they weren't tight enough. Since we tend to teach what we have been taught, I'm afraid I was guilty of teaching that concept for a while. My children still tease me about that statement.

I began studying voice at the local university. We did the opera *Der Freischütz* my freshman year and I had the role of Ännchen. This was a good role for my lyric-coloratura voice and I discovered that I loved performing. Adding to my confusion, however, my teacher—who also directed the opera—loved Wagner and the heavy German literature. He had me sing music that was wrong for my young voice, including "Voi lo sapete" from *Cavalleria Rusticana*, "Vissi d'arte" from *Tosca*, and "Liebestod" from *Tristan und Isolde* (I was 17). My voice soon had something between a bleat and a wobble, and I lost my high voice.

In addition to my vocal difficulties, I knew that I wanted a family. My husband and I were blessed with five children. I was performing with the local opera company and oratorio groups, and I soon realized that the rehearsals and performances took me away from my family too much. When we are fortunate enough to be born with a gift for singing, our dreams of having a great career as a singer seem to be part of the package. It is not always easy to keep balance in our lives in making the decision of what is most important in the grand scheme of things.

I had started teaching and really loved it, so I made the decision that I would teach rather than perform, especially with anything that required much rehearsal. My needs were completely fulfilled with teaching. It seemed like every time I performed someone would ask if I could teach them, or their daughter, or son. My studio was soon filled, although, at that time I certainly didn't feel qualified. I just tried to teach what seemed right to me based on what I had been taught. Unfortunately, the training I received was not always sound, and I had developed some very serious vocal problems. It was in trying to help my voice recover that I really became fascinated with the physiology and mechanics of the singing voice.

About the time I started teaching privately, a chapter of the National Association of Teachers of Singing was established in Utah. This organization presented some wonderful opportunities to learn from the masters. The University of Utah and NATS co-sponsored many fine, nationally prominent teachers in workshops and master classes. I started going to the national workshops and conventions. I sat on the front row with a tape recorder and notebook and learned all I could from each master teacher. Often I would ask if they would give me a private lesson so I could be sure that I understood their concepts in my own voice. I will always be grateful to the great teachers and the NATS organization for giving me the opportunity to learn.

Teaching was an ideal work-at-home career. I could work my teaching hours around my children's schedules. I'm not saying it was easy. It took lots of planning, scheduling, and cooperation from my family. I didn't start teaching at the University of Utah until my youngest son was in kindergarten, and I was able to be home when the children came home from school. My children loved my students, and in some cases they became close friends. It was really the best of both worlds.

The fact that my teaching career has lasted so many years leaves me in awe. I have had wonderful students, many of whom are singing professionally and teaching at universities and in private studios. I call my students my musical children, for I have truly loved them all. I have never taken time to count how many students I have taught, but it must be in the many hundreds.

As a result of Joseph Hoffman's scholarly paper it was suggested that I write a book about my many experiences and my general philosophy of singing and teaching. I thought it would be a compilation of the vocalises I have developed over the years along with a few thoughts and memories. I had no idea that it would turn out to be such a lengthy treatise on the art of singing. I will feel rewarded if this book is of value and inspiration to those who read it.

A dear friend gave me the following poem many years ago. I know that I made the right decision for me by choosing a teaching career rather than a singing career.

Teaching singing is such a rewarding profession. While we may indeed be rewarded in heaven for our efforts, we are already the recipients of the many rewards on earth, having had the blessing of knowing and working with wonderful people and beautiful music.

*The Jeweled Crown*

*In dream I stood near the Master,*
*To account for what I'd been given,*
*What have you done with your talents?*
*What do you bring back to Heaven?*

*I told of my long years of study,*
*Of the glory and great things I'd done,*
*I knew that my work was accepted*
*When He gave me the crown I had won.*

*As I turned then to go from His presence,*
*My eye caught a most splendid sight!*
*A crown formed of gold and of silver,*
*Studded with jewels shining light.*
*"Master," I turned back in question,*
*"To whom does this crown belong?*
*Surely, it must be for an artist—*
*But say—is it art, pen, or song?"*

*"Not so," came His quiet reply,*
*"A humble peasant was she,*
*She knew not of fortune or fame,*
*But her voice was in tune with me."*

*"Beside hers, my crown is so simple*
*And I've sung before Rulers and Kings!"*
*"I know, and thou hast thy reward*
*But you see, she taught others to sing."*

*—Lucille Harper*

159

# APPENDIX 1

## International Phonetic Alphabet (IPA) Symbols

(This is not a complete list of phonetic symbols, but those most commonly used.)

### Vowels

| Symbol | English Equivalent |
|---|---|
| [ɑ] | f<u>a</u>ther |
| [ɔ] | sh<u>a</u>wl |
| [æ] | b<u>a</u>ck |
| [e] | d<u>ay</u> |
| [ɛ] | p<u>e</u>t |
| [i] | f<u>ee</u>t |
| [ɪ] | s<u>i</u>t |
| [u] | t<u>oo</u> |
| [ʊ] | b<u>oo</u>k |
| [o] | t<u>o</u>ne |
| [ə] | sof<u>a</u> |
| [ʌ] | <u>u</u>p |

### Diphthongs

| Symbol | English Equivalent |
|---|---|
| [ɑɪ] | n<u>i</u>ght |
| [eɪ] | d<u>ay</u> |
| [ɔɪ] | b<u>oy</u> |
| [ɑu] | c<u>ow</u> |
| [ou] | s<u>o</u> |

### Triphthongs

| Symbol | English Equivalent |
|---|---|
| [ɑɪɚ] | f<u>i</u>re |
| [ɑʊɚ] | <u>ou</u>r |

### Consonants

The majority of consonant symbols, including b, d, f, g, h, k, l, m, n, p, r, s, t, v, w, and z, are identical to the English alphabet.

### Voiced

| | |
|---|---|
| [ð] | <u>th</u>ine |
| [hw] | <u>wh</u>en |
| [ʤ] | ju<u>dg</u>e |
| [ʒ] | plea<u>s</u>ure |

### Voiceless

| | |
|---|---|
| [θ] | <u>th</u>ing |
| [ʃ] | <u>sh</u>e |
| [tʃ] | <u>ch</u>arm |

### Nasal

| | |
|---|---|
| [m] | <u>m</u>any |
| [n] | <u>n</u>anny |
| [ŋ] | so<u>ng</u> |
| [ɲ] | o<u>n</u>ion |

### Semi-Vowels

| | |
|---|---|
| [j] | <u>y</u>ou |

# APPENDIX 2

## Vocal Exercises by Chapter

### 3c

**Variations**

### 4d

**Variations**

**4e**

**Variations**

**4f**

**4g**

**4h**

**Variation**

**4k**

[i]— [i]— [e]— [e]—  [i]— [i]— [e]— [e]—  [i]

**5a**

[a]————

**5b**

[ka  ka  ka  ka  ka]
[ka  la  ka  la  ka]

**5c**

[a]————————

**Variation**

[a]————————

**5d**

[a]——————

**5e**

[a]————————
(vocal fry)

165

**Variations**

**6a**

**Variation**

**6b**

**6c**

**6d**

**6e**

Bum-ble-bee  Bum-ble-bee  Bum-ble-bee  Bum-ble-bee  Bum-ble-bee  Bum-ble-bee  Bum-ble-bee  Bum-ble-bee

**6f**

[i] [i] [ɑ]   [i] [i] [ɑ]   [i] [i] [ɑ]   [i] [i] [ɑ]   [i] [i] [ɑ]
(nasal)      (nasal)      (nasal)      (nasal)      (nasal)

**6g**

[i  ɑ]  [i  ɑ]  [i  ɑ]  [i  ɑ]  [i  ɑ]

**Variations**

[i  e  ɑ]   [i  e  ɑ]   [i  e  ɑ]   [i  e  ɑ]   [i  e  ɑ]

[i    ɑ    i    ɑ    i    ɑ    i]

**6h**

[kwæ]   [kwæ][kwæ][kwæ][kwæ]  [kwæ]

**Variations**

*freely*

[kwæ ɑ]  [kwæ ɑ]  [kwæ ɑ]  [kwæ ɑ]  [kwæ ɑ]

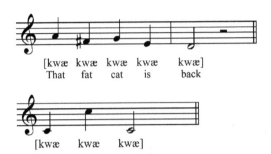

[kwæ kwæ kwæ kwæ kwæ]
That fat cat is back

[kwæ kwæ kwæ]

**7b**

[u o i e ɑ]_____

**7c**

[hʌŋ n m i u i u i u i u]_____
"hung"

**Variations**

[hʌŋ n m i u i e i u i o i u i ɑ]
"hung"

[i u i u i u i u i]_____

**7d**

Fi - glio a - mor - te
Fi - glio a - mi - te

**Variation**

Fi - glio a - mi - a - te

**7e**

What shall I sing ___ to - day?
I feel just fine ___ to - day!

**7f**

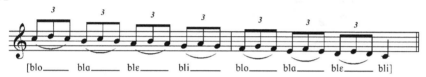

[blo___ bla___ blɛ___ bli___ blo___ bla___ blɛ___ bli]

**7g**

[prɛ prɛ prɛ prɛ prɛ]

**Variation**

[pri e ɑ] [pri e ɑ] [pri e ɑ] [pri e ɑ] [pri e ɑ]

**10a**

whoo whoo___

**Variation**

[u ɑ u] [u ɑ u] [u ɑ u] [u ɑ u] [u ɑ u]

**10b**

[i] _____ [i] _____

**Variation**

[i] _____ [e] _____ [ɑ] _____

**10c**

It's ea - sy
Ca - ro mio ben

**10d**

[mi si mi si mi]

**10e**

*legato*

[lo a mo a lo a mo a lo a] ___

**11a**

[i] [e] [ɑ]

**11b**

*staccato*

[i] [ɑ]

**11c**

[i]        [ɑ]

**11d**

[i]              [ɑ̇]

**11e**

[ɑ̇]

**11f**   messa di voce

[ɑ]

## APPENDIX 3

*In her masters scholarly paper, "Developing the Adolescent Voice in a Choral Setting: A Survey of Resources," Vicki McMurray gives some excellent evaluations on many books and articles that have been written on the adolescent voice. This is a valuable resource for choral directors. She has given me permission to use her research hoping it will be of help and save much time in finding books and articles on this subject. I am grateful to her for her willingness to share the information on this controversial subject. She researched books, professional journal articles, dissertations, and video presentations. Her survey provides an overview of resources that she considers most effective in dealing with this subject.*

### Developing the Adolescent Voice in a Choral Setting:
### A Survey of Resources
by Vicki McMurray

### Parameters for Selection of Reviewed Resources

Because adolescent vocal development has been addressed by so many, the following parameters have been set in selecting the resources to review:

The resource deals directly with adolescent vocal development in the choral setting or with concepts directly applicable to the adolescent. There are many fine sources dealing with the solo voice, the adult voice, or the child's voice, but these are not included in this survey.

There are two types of resources reviewed: 1) Sources that deal with one or more aspects of adolescent vocal development as the exclusive content; or 2) sources that are broader in scope, addressing many of the needs of the choral educator, of which this is only one of the topics addressed.

With one exception the sources are published since 1970. Choral music education has evolved significantly since that time. This is due to such factors as the Tanglewood Symposium of 1967 that sought to examine the status of and establish new directions for music education, the emergence of thought represented by Bennett Reimer's *A Philosophy of Music Education* published in 1970, and the first independent national convention of the American Choral Directors Association convened in 1971. The resources reviewed here reflect the expansion of choral music education, and in turn, the ideas regarding singing for the adolescent.

While several have been considered, most journal articles have not been included in this survey. In general, articles are not as effective in covering the subject matter because they are not as in-depth and complete. In some cases, articles are authored by those who ultimately wrote books about the subject that are more comprehensive.

Some thought has also been given to the accessibility of the resource. Generally they are commercially available or obtainable through the university library system.

## Purpose of Survey

One purpose for this survey is to act as a filter for the reader by providing a list of the sources that are most effective in dealing with this topic. It also attempts to offer a comparative look at these sources in two ways: 1) by reading the individual reviews, or 2) through a comparative table.

Finally, an underlying philosophical premise of this survey is that every person should be able to sing confidently within a group setting. Singing is a learned behavior that should be enjoyed by all, not just by an elite few of the "talented." Usually adolescence, particularly early adolescence, is the last chance to positively impact a person's image of himself as a "singer." Because of this, it is critical that the teaching of singing and developing the singing voice of the adolescent be done as effectively as possible. There is a great deal of thought, research, and experience from which to learn. This survey attempts to provide the reader with a view of the best of that information in order to bring the incomparable act of singing to all.

The following list of books and videos are those recommended most highly. This is not a complete list of those in the scholarly paper.

## Videos

Adams, Charlotte. *Daily Workout for a Beautiful Voice*. Santa Barbara, CA: Santa Barbara Music Co, 1991.

> The entire video is devoted to vocal development of the singer, utilizing a high-school girls choir to demonstrate the exercises. It is particularly useful to watch the workout video to see the accompanying movement to the

exercises. The booklet not only provides a printed record of the exercises, but other useful information in understanding and using these ideas.

It is valuable to watch and consider a careful, well-thought-out approach and accompanying movement ideas for vocal warm-ups. Watching this demonstration stimulates thought about the five areas of emphasis, which can, if adapted for one's own use, improve the vocal production of the singer. However, it does not address any of the specific problems associated with the young male singer.

Haasemann, Frauke and James M. Jordan. *Group Vocal Techniques: A Video.* Chapel Hill, NC: Hinshaw Music, Inc., 1991. (Book and video to be used together.)

This series is singular in its breadth and volume of quality, immediately applicable ideas. The combination of book, video, and vocalise cards provides the choral director with an almost inexhaustible collection of strategies for developing the voices of choir members. It focuses on connecting singing to everyday activities, making it easy and fun for the adolescent to grasp.

These resources are among the most important and valuable reviewed and would help any choral director of adolescents better meet the needs of the singers in developing their singing voices.

Leck, Henry. *The Boy's Changing Voice: Take the High Road.* Milwaukee, WI: Hal Leonard, 2001.

The entire video is devoted to the critical topic of dealing with adolescent vocal production. Much of the presentation contains footage of solo and choral performances, including warm-ups and vocal exercises. One of its greatest strengths is seeing the work in action and not just reading about it, providing an effective model of working with an adolescent boy's voice. Guidelines for voice classification and technical data are also presented.

This is a very useful and informative video for those working with the changing voice, presenting Leck's well-established and successful philosophy (the unchanged and/or high voice is essential to the development of the new voice). The footage of the vocal folds and the interviews could also be helpful for the singers to watch, making this a valuable tool for both teacher and student.

**Books**

Barham, Terry J. *Strategies for Teaching Junior High and Middle School Male Singers: Master Teachers Speak.* Santa Barbara, CA: Santa Barbara Music Publishing, 2001.

The majority of this volume deals with vocal development of the adolescent boy. It offers extensive information regarding testing and vocal ranges, which is essential to understand when working with male students at the junior high level. The section of vocalises is also extensive in providing specific suggestions for a variety of concerns such as bringing the head voice downward, breath management, and range extension. It is very interesting to see the various approaches of the participating teachers, which help to provide a very comprehensive treatment of this topic.

This is an excellent resource on this topic as well as the others it addresses. The extensive repertoire lists provide additional repertoire to that offered in his previous book. The selected bibliography contains only quality, select sources. The vocalise section is particularly valuable for immediate practical application.

Barham, Terry J., and Darolyne L. Nelson. *The Boy's Changing Voice: New Solutions for Today's Choral Teacher.* Miami, FL: Warner Bros Publications U.S., Inc., 1991.

In dealing with vocal development, this book gives solid recommendations. However, Dr. Barham's later work, *Strategies for Teaching Junior High & Middle School Male Singers: Master Teachers Speak,* is more extensive and scholarly in that regard. There are five or six vocalises printed for each of the following categories.

> Voice placement and testing
> Creating a sage and positive environment
> Selecting and adapting music and repertoire ideas
> Vocalises for vocal development
> Ideas for interacting with this age group

The information in this book is of high quality and is both practical and useful. It addresses the realities of dealing with this age group in general. While it touches on many topics, the treatment is quite brief in most cases.

Collins, Don L. *Teaching Choral Music.* 2nd ed. Upper Saddle River, NJ: Prentice-Hall, Inc, 1999.

An entire chapter is devoted to vocal technique with solid information regarding posture, breathing, and resonance, with vocalises, ideas, and explanations. Two chapters address the changing voice, from historical and practical perspectives. Another chapter deals in part with vowel and consonant production.

This is an excellent comprehensive choral methods textbook, with excellent information regarding adolescents' vocal development. It is one of the finest resources of its kind.

Cooksey, John M. *Working with Adolescent Voices.* St. Louis, MO: Concordia Publishing House, 1992.

Understanding the changing voice is essential for the choral director working with adolescent voices. Cooksey's work with the male voice advocates an eclectic approach of the theories espoused by experts Irvin Cooper, Frederick Swanson, and Duncan McKenzie. He also cites important research done with the female voice and makes recommendations based on that research. The section regarding exercising the voice is quite extensive, giving specific suggestions in the areas of posture, breathing, kinesthetics, and vocalises especially effective for the adolescent voice.

This book is very accessible to the reader, practical in its content, and one of the best resources for anyone working with the changing adolescent voice.

Cooper, Irvin, and Karl O. Kuersteiner. *Teaching Junior High School Music.* Conway, AR: Cambiata Press, 1973.

Irvin Cooper's work is important to understand with regard to the changing voice. This strategy, known as the "cambiata" approach, has been widely employed in American vocal education. It identifies four types of boys' voices that exist in grades 4-12: 1) the unchanged voice; 2) boys in the first stage of change, called cambiata; 3) boys in the second stage of change, called baritone; and 4) boys' changed voices, called basses. He maintains that 90 percent of all boys' voices change according to the same pattern—first change in seventh grade, second change in eighth grade, with tenor and bass voices beginning to appear in ninth grade.

This book is valuable as a model of sequential teaching of music concepts important on a junior-high level. Cooper's work with the changing voice is considered by many to be quite important when trying to gain a full understanding of the boy's changing voice and varying approaches to the problems associated with it. It can then be compared with other leaders in the field, enabling the educator to develop a philosophy that works in any given situation.

Haasemann, Frauke, and James M. Jordan. *Group Vocal Technique*, Chapel Hill, NC: Hinshaw Music, Inc., 1991.

(Book and video to be used together.)
See full annotation under "Videos."

Phillips, Kenneth H. *Directing the Choral Music Program.* New York: Oxford University Press, 2004.

The chapter "Working with Adolescent Singers" deals with the nature of adolescents, the female and male voice changes, and appropriate part voicings. It summarizes research in these areas by other experts in the field, providing a clear and understandable explanation of the large body of research. Fifty-five pages of the text are devoted to vocal development and warm-ups that develop vocal skills. An outline is suggested for planning a systematic process of vocal-skill development including energizing the body, breath, ear, and voice.

Phillips is a leading authority on the development of the young singer. Of the volumes that deal with a variety of topics, this is among the most valuable and highest quality in its scholarly, yet accessible content.

Phillips, Kenneth H. *Teaching Kids To Sing.* New York: Schirmer Books, 1996.

The entire book is devoted to vocal development of the young singer and can be applied in the choral setting. Phillips admits that the book employs a "cookbook" approach to vocal education. He offers a method for music teachers that tells them where to begin and what to do each step of the way. It can be utilized by the beginning teacher in its entirety or can be used selectively to supplement an existing approach.

This is a definitive work for the topics at hand. If a teacher could only have one resource, this "bible" could be the most important one.

# BIBLIOGRAPHY

Alderson, Richard. *Complete Handbook of Voice Training*. Nyack, NY: Parker Publishing Company, 1979.

Appelman, D. Ralph. *The Science of Vocal Pedagogy*. Bloomington, IN: Indiana University Press, 1967.

Balk, H. Wesley. *The Complete Singer-Actor: Training for Music Theater*. 2nd ed. Minneapolis: University of Minnesota Press, 1985.

Barlow, Wilfred. *The Alexander Principle*. London: Camelot Press Ltd, 1973.

Bartholomew, W.T. "The Role of Imagery in Voice Teaching." *MTNA Volume of Proceedings*, 1935.

Bernac, Pierre. *The Interpretation of French Song*. New York: W. W. Norton, 1978.

Boone, Daniel R. *The Voice and Voice Therapy*. Englewood Cliffs, NJ: Prentice-Hall, 1971.

Brodnitz, Friedrich S. *Keep Your Voice Healthy*. New York: Harper & Brothers, 1953.

Brown, William Earl. *Vocal Wisdom: Maxims of Giovanni Battista Lamperti*. New York: Arno Press, Inc., 1931. Enlarged ed., edited by Lillian Strongin, 1968.

Brown, Oren L. "Principles of Voice Therapy as Applied to Teaching." *NATS Bulletin* 9, no. 5 (1953): 16, 21.

_____. "Causes of Voice Strain in Singing." *NATS Bulletin* 15, no. 2 (1958): 20-21, 30.

_____. *Discover Your Voice*. San Diego: Singular Publishing Group, 1996.

Burgen, John. *Teaching Singing*. Metuchen, NJ: Scarecrow Press, 1973.

Castel, Nico. *Opera Libretti Series*. 21 vols. Genesio, NY: Leyerle Publications, 2002.

Clippinger, D.A. *The Clippinger Class Method of Voice Culture*. Philadelphia: Oliver Ditson, 1932.

Coffin, Berton, Ralph Errolle, Werner Singer, and Pierre Delattre. *Phonetic Readings of Songs and Arias*. Boulder, CO: Pruett Press, 1964.

Coffin, Berton, Werner Singer, and Pierre Delattre. *Word-By-Word Translations of Songs and Arias, Part I: German and French*. New York: Scarecrow Press, 1966.

David, Laurence E. "An Interview with Judith Stransky, Alexander Teacher." *Bulletin of Structural Integration* 2, no. 1 (1970): 5-11.

Dewhurst-Maddock, Olivea. *The Book of Sound Therapy*. New York: Simon & Schuster, Inc., 1993

DeYoung, Richard. *The Singer's Art*. Foreword by I.A. Richards. Chicago: DePaul University, 1958.

Drake, Jonathan. *Body Know How*. London: Thorsons, 1991.

Feldenkrais, M. *Awareness Through Movement*. New York: Harper & Row, 1972.

Fields, Victor A. *Training the Singing Voice: An Analysis of the Working Concepts Contained in Recent Contributions to Vocal Pedagogy*. New York: King's Crown Press, 1947.

_____. *Foundation of the Singer's Art*. New York: Vantage Press, 1977.

Forward, Geoffrey. *American Diction For Singers*. 1st ed. rev. with Elisabeth Howard. Los Angeles: Forward Company, 1994.

Gallwey, W.T. *The Inner Game of Tennis.* New York: Random House, 1976.

Garcia, Manuel. *Hints on Singing.* Original work published in 1894. New York: Patelson's House of Music, 1982.

Gardini, Nellie. *Porpora Vocal Technique: A Guide for Singers and Speakers.* Coral Gables, FL: S and G Library, Inc., 1967.

Goldman, Jonathan. *The 7 Secrets of Sound Healing.* Carlsbad, CA: Hay House, Inc., 2008

Gregg, Jean Westerman. "On the ASHA-NATS Joint Statement on Voice Therapy for Singers." *The NATS Journal* 50, Nov/Dec (1993): 49-50.

Grubb, Thomas. *Singing in French.* New York: Schirmer, 1979.

Head, Michael. "Sweet Chance That Led My Steps Abroad." Poem by W. H. Davies. High Key. Boosey & Hawkes, 1929.

Herbert-Caesari, Edgar F. *The Science and Sensations of Vocal Tone.* Boston: Crescendo Publishing Company, 1971.

_____. *The Voice of the Mind.* Boston: Crescendo Publishing Company, 1971.

_____. *Vocal Truth.* Boston: Crescendo Publishing Company, 1969.

Hollein, Harry. "A Report on Vocal Registers." *Transcripts of the Symposium, Care of the Professional Voice, Part 1.* New York: The Voice Foundation, 1983.

Jahn, Anthony. "Vocal Health: Oral Contraceptives and the Voice." *Classical Singer* 16, no. 2 (2003): 14.

_____. "Seasonal Allergies: A Strategy for Survival." *Classical Singer* 18, no. 7 (2005): 16.

Kagen, Sergius. *On Studying Singing.* New York: Rinehart & Company, Inc., 1950. Reprint, New York: Dover, 1960.

Large, John, and Shigenobu Iwata. "The Significance of Air Flow Modulations in Vocal Vibrato." *The NATS Bulletin* 32, no. 3, (1976): 42-7.

Lehmann, Lilli. *How to Sing.* Translated by Richard Aldrich. New York: Macmillan, 1902. New rev. and supplemented ed. translated by Clara Willenbücher. Mineola, NY: Dover, 1993.

Lehmann, Lotte. *More than Singing: The Interpretation of Songs.* New York: Boosey & Hawkes Inc., 1945. Reprint, Mineola, NY: Dover, 1985.

Lessac, Arthur. *The Use and Training of the Human Voice: A Practical Approach to Speech and Voice Dynamics.* 2nd ed. Mountain View, CA: Mayfield Publishing Company, 1967.

LeVan, Timothy. *Masters of the Italian Art Song: Word-By-Word and Poetic Translations of the Complete Songs for Voice and Piano.* Metuchen, NJ: Scarecrow Press, 1990.

Linklater, Kristin. *Freeing the Natural Voice.* New York: Drama Book Specialists, 1976.

Maisel, Edward, ed. *The Resurrection of the Body: The Writings of F. Matthias Alexander.* New York: University Books, 1969.

Meryman, Richard. "A Tour of Two Great Throats." *Life,* June 26, 1970.

McKinney, J.C. *The Diagnosis and Correction of Vocal Faults.* Nashville: Broadman Press, 1982.

Miller, Richard. *Techniques of Singing.* Metuchen, NJ: Scarecrow Press, 1977.

_____. *The Structure of Singing: System and Art in Vocal Technique.* New York: Schirmer Books, 1986.

Miller, Phillip L. *The Ring of the Words: An Anthology of Song Texts*. New York: W.W. Norton & Company, 1965.

Murdock, Ron. "Born to Sing." In *Curiosity Recaptured: Exploring the Ways We Think and Move*, ed. by Jerry Sontag, 135-162. San Francisco: Mornum Time Press, 1996.

Nuland, Sherwin B. *Leonardo da Vinci*. New York: Viking Penguin, 2000.

Prawer, S.S. *The Penguin Book of Lieder*. Baltimore: Penguin Press, 1964.

Schoep, Arthur, and Daniel Harris. *Word-by-Word Translations of Songs and Arias, Part 2: Italian*. Metuchen, NJ: Scarecrow Press, 1972.

Reid, Cornelius L. *The Free Voice*. New York: The Joseph Patelson Music House, 1965.

_____. *Bel Canto*. New York: The Joseph Patelson Music House, 1972.

Report of the Committee On The Solo Voice and Choral Singing National Association of Teachers of Singing. "The Solo Voice and Choral Singing." Published in a paper in the NATS *Internos* (now called the *Journal of Singing*).

Ristad, Eloise. *A Soprano on Her Head*. Moab, UT: Real People Press, 1982.

Sataloff, Robert T. "Professional Singers: The Science and Art of Clinical Care." *American Journal of Otolaryngology* 2, no. 3 (1981): 251-66.

Vennard, William. *Singing: The Mechanism and the Technic* [sic]. New York: Carl Fischer, Inc., 1967.

# INDEX

NOTES

CPSIA information can be obtained
at www.ICGtesting.com
Printed in the USA
BVHW011813220120
569858BV00022B/177